154.63

DREAMS
&Destinies

The Mysteries of Your Dreams Explained

BERYL BEARE

JG
PRESS

For Duncan and Stuart

Published in the USA 1995 by JG Press
Distributed by World Publications, Inc.

The JG Press Imprint is a Trademark of
JG Press, Inc.
455 Somerset Avenue
North Dighton, MA 02764

Designed and produced by
Touchstone
Old Chapel Studio, Plain Road
Marden, Tonbridge Kent TN12 9LS
United Kingdom

ISBN 1-5721-5125-0

Printed in Great Britain

Photography Credits:

(*Abbreviations: r = right, l = left, t = top, b = below*)

The Image Bank: Front and back cover – large picture;
pages 1, 4, 5, 16, 30(*b*), 32, 33, 34, 36, 37, 39, 40, 41, 43, 44,
46(*b*), 47(*t*), 48, 49, 50, 51, 52, 55, 56(*r*), 58, 59, 61, 62, 63(*t*),
64(*t*), 65, 66, 67, 68, 69, 70, 71, 72, 73, 75(*l & tr*), 76, 77(*b*),
78(*b*), 80, 81, 82, 83(*b*), 84, 85, 86, 87, 88, 89, 90(*t*), 91, 92, 93, 94.
Images Colour Library Ltd: pages 6, 7, 9, 10, 11, 12, 13,
14, 15, 17, 18, 19, 20, 21, 22, 23, 24, 25, 26, 27, 28, 29, 30, 31,
35, 38, 42, 45, 46(*t*), 47(*b*), 53, 54, 56(*l*), 57, 63(*b*), 64(*b*), 74,
75(*b*), 77(*t*), 78(*t*), 83(*t*), 90(*l & b*).
The Bridgeman Art Library: Front cover, centre picture.

Contents

Introduction

Begin a voyage of discovery.
Explore your dreams and
interpret the messages that
they have for you.

Imagine you are going to spend one third of the next year in a strange country. Almost certainly, you will try to find out as much about it as you can. You will probably consult guide books and maps, and check on such things as travel, climate and language.

Yet we spend approximately one third of our life asleep, and know so little about the intriguing world of our dreams!

Once we begin to understand this strange world, we also begin to understand hitherto unknown aspects of our own personality. And the voyage of discovery is not restricted to those who claim that they 'always dream'. We all dream, every night. It is only the extent to which we recall our dreams that varies.

Now you have the opportunity to improve your recall, explore your dreams and learn something of their language. Most importantly, you will be able to interpret the messages that they have for you, personally.

Dream Discovery

The first part of this book takes you on a journey through the history of dreams and their meanings world-wide. Sleep and dreaming is then dealt with more scientifically, and some of the theories of Freud and Jung are explained.

In the Dream Workshop you will discover how to recall your dreams more successfully, and how they can help you to solve problems and improve creativity. The Dream Library then gives you information about almost every aspect of dreaming, with samples of actual dreams.

Dream Themes

The second part of the book, Themes and Meanings, is your guide map to personal interpretation. This is an accessible route to understanding dreams, because it enables you to explore the whole of your dream rather than just a single object, or symbol.

Having dreamt of a telephone (say), and consulted the Themes and Meanings contents list on page 55, you will look under 'Communication' and find your dream. But seeing 'Colours' also in the contents list may remind you that the telephone was yellow, and lead you on to further exploration – and discovery. Or you may find that other dreams under the same theme also have some relevance, and 'nudge' your recall that little bit further.

Now you're really travelling. Journey well – the rewards are truly worth while!

Once we begin to understand this strange world, we also begin to understand hitherto unknown aspects of our own personality.

The Mystery of Dreams

Macbeth's three witches predict that he will become King (above). Through history, great significance has also been given to supernatural dreams predicting the future.

Dreams have always fascinated us. Throughout history we have sought to unravel their mysteries and to interpret their meanings. At one time they were thought to be of divine origin – messages from the gods – and were received as warnings or prophecies sent for the dreamer's guidance.

They were frequently received in the form of symbols and images, much as our dreams are today, and professional interpreters were required to decipher them. Such an interpreter was the Greek Artemidorus, author of the most famous dream book of the ancient world, the *Oneirocritica* (*The Interpretation of Dreams*). Written in the 2nd century AD, it ran to five volumes, was published in English for the first time in the mid 17th century and was so popular that by 1722 it had already reached 20 editions.

Many of Artemidorus' interpretations will sound odd to us today, yet in some ways he was surprisingly modern. He specified the importance of the dreamer's personality in dream analysis and noted the frequency of sexual symbols. He was also very aware of the tricks that dreams can play, including the use of puns, and many of his interpretations seem to anticipate the concepts of Freud and Jung.

Looking Back

Long before Artemidorus, the ancient Egyptians and the Assyrians also had their dream books. In the library of King Assurbanipal of Assyria there were books of dream interpretations believed to have dated from 2000BC, and the king's personal dream book was probably one of Artemidorus' chief sources of inspiration.

In medieval times, dreams could serve as a sanction for those wishing to put forward radical policies and political programmes. The knight who informed King Henry II that the voices of St Peter and the Archangel Gabriel had told him to present a number of demands foreshadowing Magna Carta is an example.

Throughout the ages, dreams seem to have provided people with the authority to take decisions, engage in controversial acts and identify criminals. The case of Maria Marten of the Red Barn is just one of the

murder mysteries resolved when the culprit was denounced on the basis of a dream.

Mrs Marten dreamed that her daughter had been murdered and buried in the Red Barn. The barn was searched, and Maria's body discovered. William Corder, who had maintained the girl was with him in Ipswich, was hanged for the crime on 11 August 1828.

Dreams and the Supernatural

Belief in the supernatural significance of vivid and recurring dreams had been kept alive by the early Church. In the 16th century some importance was still attached to dreams, although theologians declared that most had physical causes and should be ignored. However, they did admit that some dreams might be supernaturally inspired, though as likely to be diabolical as divine – and even more likely to be the effects of indigestion.

Some connection between magic and holiness was certainly presumed by a majority of people, and dream interpretation was one of the services performed by wizards and astrologers for their clients. One example of the way in which they 'procured' prophetic dreams was the placing of objects under a young girl's pillow, so that she might see her future husband in her sleep.

Magic played little part in the Victorian attitude to dreams. They found them most disturbing, and were particularly distressed by sexual dreams. It was into this climate that Sigmund Freud launched his famous book *The Interpretation of Dreams* (published 1900). There was already extensive literature on the subject, but with his exploration of the unconscious it could be said that Freud was largely responsible for pulling the threads together.

A devil reduced to servitude.
Fifteen Century.

Witches also performed dream interpretation.

Famous Dreams

Were the famous visionaries of the past really dreaming, or were they receiving divine inspiration in a trance-like state other than sleep? Most of the visions and revelations which were so common just before the Restoration (1665) were probably what we should call dreams, and prophets – as well as poets – have not infrequently spoken of 'dreaming of a vision'. So the dividing line between the two is obviously fragile.

Although prophetic dreaming was fairly common in the ancient world, it was not without its dissenters. Aristotle (who joined Plato's academy at Athens in 367BC) dismissed such dreams as mere coincidences, and the Roman orator Cicero 'repudiated the arts of divination', which amounts to the same thing.

The Bible is full of dreams of divination, one of the most famous being Jacob's Ladder. Travelling to Pandanaram, Jacob broke his journey at nightfall and lay down on a pillow of stones to sleep. He dreamed of a ladder reaching from earth to heaven, on which angels moved up and down. Awakening, he recognized at once that the dream was divine and was able to interpret it. 'This is none other than the house of God,' he declared, 'and this is the gate of heaven,' (Gen.28.17).

Jacob's dream. "And he dreamed, and behold a ladder set up on the earth, and the top of it reached to heaven: and behold the angel of God ascending and descending on it. . ." Genesis 28:12)

The Forgotten Dream

King Nebuchadnezzar had less skill than Jacob in the power of interpretation or, indeed, of recall. He summoned magicians, astrologers and sorcerers to 'shew' him his dream. 'I have dreamed a dream,' he said, 'and my spirit was troubled to know the dream,' (Dan.2.3).

When the assembled magicians asked him to tell them what the dream was, the king replied that it was gone from him but that he still required them to interpret it. If they could not do so, their houses would be destroyed and they would be slain.

Daniel's dream vision is generally accepted as an example of divination.

A Night Vision

Daniel, a prophet and Jewish exile in Babylon (to whom *The Book of Daniel* is credited), was among the magicians. He pleaded for time and returned to his house to sleep. While he slept his dreams were propitious. 'Then was the secret revealed unto Daniel in a night vision.' (Dan.2.19)

He returned to the king and was able to give him an interpretation of his dream, thus saving the day, his life and the lives of his colleagues. Daniel's dream vision is generally accepted as an example of divination, but that does not alter the fact that the dream-within-a-dream which he experienced is very similar to lucid dreaming as we know it today.

Joseph was also the recipient of a number of biblical dream visions. In one, an angel of the Lord appeared to assure him of his wife's chastity.

Many women were certainly prophetic dreamers, and if they made little impact as visionaries it was through no fault of their own, but rather because they were taken less seriously.

While Pilate was sitting in judgement of Jesus, his wife sent word to him saying, 'I have nothing to do with that just man: for I have suffered many things this day in a dream because of him,' (Math.27.19). However, she was ignored.

Muhammad

The prophet Muhammad received his divine calling in a vision. In early middle age he experienced the promptings of the one god, Allah, and from that time seems to have received many revelations, or visions.

The visions involved the angel Gabriel reading the divine messages from a book. Muhammad himself was unable to read or write and so he had his wife Khadijah record them for him. They are now preserved in the *Qu'ran*, and because that is considered a true copy of the Heavenly Book, cannot be questioned.

Joseph interpreting the dream.

Dante had a vision of the circles of Heaven.

Dreams in Art and Literature

In Greek and Latin literature, dreams were often represented as beings. Hesiod, who in 700BC was one of the earliest Greek poets, called them the Daughters of Night. In Homer's *Odyssey*, however, they lived near the gates of the sun.

Later poets wrote of Morpheus, a god of dreams (hence 'morphia' and 'morphine'), who made human shapes appear to dreamers. And in the *Aeneid*, Virgil (70-19BC) says that the spirits of the dead send dreams from the Underworld – true dreams through a gate of horn, and false dreams through a gate of ivory.

The Greek author Plutarch, whose writings were a source for many of Shakespeare's plays, makes the distinction between pleasant dreams and 'strange and absurd visions'. He likens the former to rays of light rebounding from a good philosophy, and the latter to broken waves beating upon the rocks and craggy banks of the shore.

Writers, artists and musicians have always dreamed vividly, so it is hardly surprising that dream images have appeared frequently in their work. One musician who had a particularly active dream life was Richard Wagner. He remembered most of his dreams in detail and related them to his wife, who recorded them in her diaries.

Titania, Queen of the Fairies, lying asleep. From William Shakespeare's A Midsummer Night's Dream.

The Flying Dutchman

Vivid and compelling dreams greatly influenced Wagner's 'Music Drama' and played a central part in his works for the stage. So much so, that one director of *The Flying Dutchman* was persuaded to interpret the whole action of the opera as a dream.

Wagner's second wife, Cosima, recorded his dreams meticulously, and in doing so provided us with a more complete dream record than we have for any other artist of the past. We know that Wagner dreamed lucidly, that he had anxiety dreams and, above all, that he was besieged by 'the most wanton and sumptuous fantasies'.

He was ill, he had nightmares. He suffered. But occasionally, a kinder dream would bring him some sort of comfort. In January 1877, Cosima reported that he had a reasonable night with a pleasant dream about his old parrot, 'which came flying back to him calling "Richard", and singing him melodies from his works.'

Dreams and Visions in Art

Many graphic artists have also been greatly affected by dreams. The French symbolist Odilon Redon (1840-1916) worked largely in charcoal and pastels. His aim was to give dramatic visual form to half forgotten dreams and anxieties, not to represent reality. His first album of lithographs appeared in 1879, under the appropriate title *In Dream*.

His symbolism varies between imaginative or 'dream' imagery, and literary sources. In his charcoal drawings of the 1880s, known as the *Noirs*, he takes his inspiration from literature and draws on the works of Shakespeare, Poe, Flaubert and Baudelaire.

Later, in 1891, he was to produce a fine album called simply, *Dreams*. Here, he moves away from literary sources altogether, and blends religious and related subjects in a deliberately confusing way that is synonymous with dreaming.

Victor Hugo, French poet, novelist and dramatist (1802-85) is remembered mainly for such literary achievements as *Les Miserables* and *Notre Dame de Paris*. But he was also a very talented graphic artist with numerous fine drawings to his credit. One of these, *The Dream*, shows a disembodied arm with the hand stretching upwards, and its concentration upon a single symbolic image foreshadows some of Redon's work.

Literature, of course, is full of dreams. One only has to think of such creations as Frankenstein, Jekyll and Hyde, the nightmare qualities of most of Edgar Allan Poe's stories, or the dream-like imagery in much of Kafka's writing.

Nightmare qualities are apparent in many works of art, music and literature.

Shakespeare

The plays of Shakespeare abound in dreams, but we do not know if any were taken from his own experiences. Like most artists he probably dreamed vividly, so it seems reasonable to suppose that, directly or indirectly, some of his dream-life found its way into his work.

He uses dreams in many different ways. Prophetically – if with tongue in cheek – in *A Midsummer Night's Dream*, when Hermia is terrified by a nightmare. She dreams that a serpent is eating her heart away while her lover, Lysander, smiles uncaringly. On waking she discovers that Lysander has, indeed, deserted her.

Shakespeare also uses dreams disturbingly, as in *Richard III*, when Clarence vividly relates his dream of drowning. The horror of the dream, he says, remains with him long after he wakes. In *Julius Caesar* there is irony in the warning dream. Caesar tells

how his wife, Calphurnia, dreamed of his statue spouting blood and begged him to stay at home. Unfortunately he tells his dream to Decius, who is one of the conspirators against him. A quick thinker, Decius replies that the dream has been misinterpreted and, in fact, bodes good fortune!

Comedy and the Absurd

Shakespeare is a great user of puns and comedy, and he employs these in dreams, too. Bottom's amazed reaction to his ass-headed 'dream' (*A Midsummer Night's Dream*) is, of course, unequivocally comic. Romeo's exchange with his friend Mercutio (*Romeo and Juliet*) is an example of pun dreaming.

> *Romeo:* I dreamed a dream last night.
> *Mercutio:* And so did I.
> *Romeo:* Well, what was yours?
> *Mercutio:* That dreamers often lie.

It shall be called 'Bottom's Dream', because it hath no bottom.

William Shakespeare, *A Midsummer Night's Dream.*

Franz Kafka's account of a dream in his *Diaries* (1911) evokes that feeling of absurdity familiar to many of us in our dreams. 'I dreamed that Max, Otto and I had the habit of packing our trunks only when we reached the railway station. There we were, carrying our shirts, for example, through the main hall to our distant trunks.'

Moving Images

In Kafka's short story *A Dream*, the protagonist, Josef K, visits a cemetery and finds himself on a moving path, 'gliding along as if on a rushing stream.' He wants to pause by a certain grave-mound and finds himself almost leaving it behind. 'He made a hasty spring on to the grass. But since the path went rushing on under his shifting foot, he tottered and fell on his knees . . .'

Most of us have experienced something of this incongruity in our dreams. We find ourselves at our destination without having made any effort to get there, or we find ourselves somewhere different altogether, but in the dream situation we accept this as our destination anyway.

Lewis Carroll makes brilliant use of this dream absurdity in *Alice's Adventures in Wonderland* and *Alice Through the Looking Glass*. '"Are we nearly there?" Alice managed to pant out at last. "Nearly there!" the Queen repeated. "Why, we passed it ten minutes ago! Faster!"' The books are, of course, intended as children's stories, but much of the dream imagery and symbolism remains relevant to us in adulthood.

Kubla Kahn

Many writers have been inspired by dreams. Coleridge (1772-1834) maintained that the lines for his poem *Kubla Kahn* came to him in a dream, although some recent scholars have questioned the accuracy of this.

Charles Dickens, writing a letter to a friend in 1843, states quite categorically, 'I never dream of any of my own characters, and I feel that it is so impossible I would wager Scott never did of his, real as they are'.

Authors have certainly been known to dream of characters before writing about them. Mary Shelley saw Frankenstein's 'monster' in a dream, or night vision, and subsequently created what is possibly the most famous Gothic horror story in the world.

From Arthur Rackham's illustration to Alice's Adventures in Wonderland.

Great Dreams of Mythology

The Greek demon Malacoda.

According to Jung, the archetypal images of myth and dream are 'psychic structures' which are common to us all, and form what he calls the collective unconscious. These mythological dreams, drawing upon human experience from time immemorial, he refers to as the 'Great' dreams.

In ancient Greece the word *mythos* (from which our word myth is derived) meant a saying, or a story. However, the Greek Euhemerus (300BC), put forward the theory that there is an element of historical truth in myths, and that the mythical gods were only kings and other heroes who were given the honour of deification by the people.

Myths have provided primitive peoples with an explanation for laws, customs and the order of things generally. They also appear to embody universal values, or patterns, with regard to human psychology. The child's relationship to its parents in terms of the Oedipus myth is an example of this.

Cultural mythologies from Egypt, Greece, and Rome, and in Hinduism have given us the material for most of the world's greatest art and literature. But it is an Assyrian poem, *The Epic of Gilgamesh*, that portrays the first tragic hero of whom anything is known.

The Dreams of Gilgamesh

The epic poem narrating the life of King Gilgamesh of Uruk, Mesopotamia, ranks as the first written literature of any consequence. The tablets on which is was recorded were discovered during the last century. The poem dates from the third millennium BC, and after five thousand years is still remarkable for its universality and enduring appeal.

The Epic of Gilgamesh is a mixture of adventure, morality and tragedy. It is punctuated by the dreams of both the hero, Gilgamesh, and Enkidu, who becomes his great friend. In Gilgamesh's first dream Enkidu is symbolized by a meteor falling from heaven. In his second dream, Gilgamesh finds an axe to which he is mysteriously drawn and this, too, symbolizes the arrival of Enkidu.

Gilgamesh induces the dreams that he and Enkidu experience during their adventures, and when Enkidu dies, Gilgamesh wanders far and wide in his grief. He searches for the secret of immortality and, according to the legend, almost succeeds in finding it.

The epic concludes with the death of Gilgamesh in his own city. 'He was wise, he saw mysteries and knew secret things . . . He went on a long journey, was weary worn out with labour, and returning engraved on a stone the whole story.'

Penelope's Dream

Gilgamesh's dreams were represented symbolically and needed interpreting. Dreams also played a very important part in the *Iliad* and the *Odyssey*, both written by the Greek epic poet Homer (probably in the eighth century BC). The dream messages in these mythological poems were not presented in symbols and therefore interpretation was seldom necessary.

In the *Odyssey*, Homer relates the dream of Penelope, wife of Odysseus and mother of Telemachus. Odysseus is believed lost, and in his absence Penelope is troubled by a number of suitors. She hears that the suitors plan to murder Telemachus who has sailed away in search of his father. Penelope is distraught and prays to the goddess Athene to intervene and save her son.

Penelope has a sister, and the goddess chooses to take her form when she appears to Penelope in a dream. We are given no explanation for this subterfuge, but doubtless Athene has her reasons. She assures Penelope that her son will be safe, protected by the powerful Athene herself.

Penelope then asks her 'sister' if she has any message as to the whereabouts of Odysseus. 'Is he alive somewhere . . . or is he dead by now and down in Hades Halls?' But Athene, eschewing sisterly solicitude, refuses to be drawn further and leaves.

The King of Hell in Hades.

Native American Myths

In the mythologies of the Native Americans there is no place of punishment, neither do their deities show any particular malevolence toward humanity. They do, however, present two quite different views of supernatural life. One is the destination of human beings after death, and the other a dwelling place for a spiritual race somewhat higher than humankind.

The myths of the Blackfoot Indians are often bizarre, and many tales are told of their creator Nápi. These mainly concern the way in which Nápi made the world and all its inhabitants.

The mythologies of the Native Americans show two very different views of supernatural life.

A Blackfoot Day-and-Night Myth

A poor Indian had a wife and two sons and they lived on nothing but roots and berries. One night, the man had a dream in which he was told to hang a large spider-web in the forest to trap animals for food.

He did this successfully, but was suspicious that his frequently absent wife was being unfaithful. Telling his two sons to flee, he spread the spider-web over the door of their hut to ensnare the woman.

The wife returned, became entangled in the meshes of the web and struggled violently. Eventually she managed to get her head through the door, whereupon her husband severed it from her shoulders with his axe.

He ran into the valley, hotly pursued by his wife's body, while her head gave chase to the two children. They, however, succeeded in outwitting and drowning it. The boys separated, one to make the white people and the other, who was called Nápi, to make the Blackfeet.

The woman's body still chases her husband. She is now the Moon and he is the Sun. If she catches and slays him, it will be night for evermore. But as long as he evades her, night and day will continue to follow one another.

The Eater of Dreams

In old Japan, evil dreams were believed to be the result of evil spirits, and a supernatural being called Baku was known as the 'Eater of Dreams'. The Baku was an extraordinary creature with a lion's face, a horse's body, the tail of a cow, the forelock of a rhinoceros – and the feet of a tiger.

Those waking from nightmares would call upon Baku to devour their dreams. And the Baku, if it could be persuaded to eat a horrible dream, had the power to change it into good fortune.

The firefly also plays an important role in Japanese mythology. In ancient times, fireflies were believed to possess medical properties. Firefly ointment was thought to be an antidote for all poisons and to have the power to drive away evil spirits and protect a house from robbers.

More recently, people would flock to Uji to see the *Hotaru-Kassen* or Firefly Battle, when all caged fireflies were released to re-enact the old clan battles of the 12th century.

A Firefly Dream

As a young man returned to his house one winter evening, a firefly flew toward him. Surprised to see it on such a cold night, he struck at it with his stick, whereupon it flew into the garden next door.

The following day he called at his neighbour's house, and was about to relate the experience with the firefly when the eldest daughter came into the room. She told the young man that the night before she had dreamt most vividly that she was a firefly.

'I saw you, and flew toward you to tell you I had learnt to fly,' she said. 'But you thrust me aside with your stick. It was really frightening!'

The eldest daughter was the young man's bride to be, so he very wisely held his peace.

Native American witch runs with the wolf.

Nightmare demons, from 'The Nightmare', Eighteenth Century.

Riding the Night Mare

In Middleton's play *The Witch* (c. 1616) the son of Hecate, the chief witch, asks his mother, 'pray give me leave to ramble abroad tonight with the Nightmare, for I have a great mind to overlay a fat parson's daughter.'

In the past, presenting the nightmare as a living entity was not uncommon. It was sometimes referred to as the 'night hag' or the 'riding of the witch'. One medieval definition of mare is, in fact, 'hag'.

The nightmare was sometimes referred to as the 'night hag' or the 'riding of the witch'.

The Grimm Brothers described it as a traveller in physical form, and speak of shepherds observing a nightmare regularly crossing a river in a boat. The shepherds stole the boat, leaving the nightmare stranded on the opposite bank. The creature was thereby reduced to a pitiful wailing, demanding that the boat be returned.

The nightmare was originally defined as a feeling of suffocation or great distress felt during sleep. Many of us will have experienced that sensation of being pressed down upon by something inexplicably frightening, and at the same time being unable to move a muscle. Some physical explanations have been put forward for this, but the findings are still inconclusive.

The Incubus

In many respects, nightmares and incubi are synonymous. The nightmare was an evil spirit and so was the incubus. The incubus, however, had strong sexual associations. It was presumed to be male (succubus is the female), but Hecate's lines in *The Witch* show there was some ambiguity here.

'What young man can we wish to
    please us
But we enjoy him in an incubus?'

The incubus was believed to settle on women to have sexual intercourse with them while they slept, and was even credited with the power to make them pregnant.

The demon known as the incubus seeks sexual relations with sleeping women. From the mid-nineteenth century, based on The Nightmare *by Fuseli.*

Night Horrors

Many people suffer from nightmares at sometime or another, but the levels of distress may vary from person to person. To some, the sensation of being suffocated, or pressed down upon, is so oppressive that there is a feeling of being literally 'taken over' or possessed.

These 'incubus' experiences provide forceful material for much of the psychological horror in films like *The Exorcist*. Yet on waking we are more inclined to think that our dream was like the film, than to acknowledge that the film may have been based on dream experiences such as our own.

The Swiss artist Fuseli was reputed to eat raw beef and pork chops for supper in order to induce the dreams that inspired many of his macabre creations. Whether they were the products of indigestion, or his obsession with horror and the supernatural, the results are certainly grotesque. In his best known painting *The Nightmare*, he depicts the subject of the title as a ghoulish equine creature.

Shakespeare's *Macbeth* was one of the sources for Fuseli's work, and in Lady Macbeth's sleep-walking scene we have an example of nightmare reflecting a state of mental breakdown.

Frankenstein

Mary Shelley's *Frankenstein* (1831) was conceived in what she recalled as a half-waking nightmare. 'I saw – with eyes shut, but with acute mental vision, – I saw the pale student of unhallowed arts kneeling beside the thing he had put together.'

A nightmare usually wakens us, yet she maintains she had not yet fallen asleep. But 'dream' or vision, it was auspicious, as she, Shelley and Byron had each undertaken to write a ghost story. 'What terrified me will terrify others; and I need only describe the spectre which had haunted my midnight pillow.'

The following day she announced she had 'thought of a story'. An announcement that was possibly the understatement of several centuries!

Coloured engraving from the first edition of Frankenstein, *1831.*

Child Nightmares

Nightmares are not uncommon during the formative years, but most children grow out of them. Night terrors tend to occur in early childhood and rarely continue beyond puberty.

Night terrors differ from nightmares in that they usually take place within about two hours of going to bed, and the child does not awake during or immediately following the experience. When the child does awake, he or she may be screaming, disoriented and quite unable to explain what is so frightening. Understandably, parents find this disturbing, as it is difficult to reassure a small child without knowing the cause of the distress. But, of course, reassurance and comfort are optimum requirements.

Nightmares, on the other hand, awaken the sleeper and remain vividly in the mind. Children will often wake up crying, and talking about the 'bad dream' can be beneficial to them. Sleepwalking also occurs with some children, and while this is worrying for parents the child nearly always grows out of it and medical attention is very seldom needed.

Demons and Monsters

A fear of the dark may cause frightening dreams in which the child is locked in an unlit room with an unidentifiable monster. Nightmares in which people turn into attacking demons, however, may indicate that the child has some difficulty with his or her own self-image. Animal nightmares – being attacked by a mad bull, for example – usually indicate frustration or anger.

Stress is an important factor in the cause of both nightmares and night terrors, so it is important to take a careful look at your child's daily life. Television bedtime viewing may be to blame. Disturbing films seen just before going to bed create greater proportions of anxiety elements during deep-sleep dreaming. Yet such films are commonly watched by even very young children.

Adult Nightmares

A nightmare will wake us by its sheer horror, and the true nightmare, or 'incubus' experience, seldom presents a visual image to explain the fear. We are conscious only of something threatening us, or bearing down upon us.

Psychoanalysts explain these dreams as emanating from great anxiety or sexual repression. In the deepest dream-sleep we are quite immobile, and this has been put forward as a physical reason for the sensation of being unable to move when experiencing such dreams.

Unpleasant dreams of varying degree may be vivid enough to recur, or they may be a 'one off'. But if they do not waken us, they are not nightmares.

Demons in Hell.

Menace of the Night

Frightening dreams can take melodramatic forms – being forced to commit a terrible crime, or being taken to the gallows, for example. Sometimes such dreams are so terrifying that we will wake up before the horror is realized. The experience will remain with us vividly, however, impressing on us the need to bring repressed desires and energies into consciousness, and to deal with them.

Often the nightmare is claustrophobic, and the dreamer is threatened with a menacing presence in a confined space, or room. This is the parallel of a child's 'monster' dream.

Recent research suggests that as many as a million adults in Britain have at least two dreams a week that are frightening enough to awaken them. And laboratory tests show that such dreams can be triggered off by a loud noise.

Nightmares of pure horror may be expressed in dreams of gory deaths and graveyard ghouls, and even cannibalism. The author Gustave Flaubert dreamt of a bloody orgy in which he was the main dish. 'The typical prisoner of nightmare, he could neither shout nor move.'

The Dreaming World

Greek myths are full of dream traditions.

Dreams are one thing that we have in common with every society in the world. The importance of dreaming is universal. Dream traditions, however, may vary considerably from culture to culture.

Among the Eskimos of Hudson Bay, for example, there is a belief that the soul leaves the body during sleep to live in a special dream world. Believers fear that if they wake someone who is sleeping, that person's soul may be lost for ever.

The people of Greenland and New Guinea also believe that the soul leaves the body during sleep, and that the adventures it encounters are related as dreams. The Zulu people have their prophetic dreamers, believing that dream messages and visions are sent to them by ancestors. The Zulu visionary who receives such messages is called a 'Dreamhouse'.

The famous Dreamtime of the Australian Aborigines, on the other hand, does not refer to dreams in the ordinary sense at all. The 'Dreaming' was the creative period at the dawn of time, when giant-like mythic beings roamed the barren countryside establishing human life. The Aborigine shares a common life-force with these mythic beings, and as part of the 'Dreaming' receives an indestructible identity for all time.

The Dreamtime

If it is not dreaming, then just what is the Aborigine Dreamtime? A myth? A blue-print for life itself? To the Aborigine it presents a unity of belief that is absolute, and while we may find it difficult to understand, few of us would deny that its simplistic beauty stirs the imagination.

The world is flat to the Aborigines, and the horizon is the end of the universe. Consequently, they fear that if they travel that far they will be in danger of falling over the edge and into bottomless space.

They believe that in the beginning the earth was quite featureless, with neither mountains, valleys nor watercourses, and was uninhabited by any living thing. Then, in the long distant past of the Dreamtime, giant semi-human beings rose from the plains where they had been slumbering and wandered aimlessly over the land. As they wandered, they performed the same tasks that the Aborigines perform today. They made fire, dug for water, fought each other and held ceremonies.

This Dreamtime suddenly and mysteriously ended, and wherever the giant creators had been active some mountain range, valley or watercourse now marks the place.

The Mystery of Creation

When asked what brought about this wonderful change, the Aborigines will reply that they do not know. They will tell you, however, that if some wise old man from an earlier time had been present, he would undoubtedly have had the answer. Nevertheless, they accept that the Dreamtime giants made everything with which they are in daily contact, and from which they gain their livelihood.

Aborigine myths can be compared with those of the ancient civilizations of the world. In Greece, for example, gods and demi-gods of Olympia were credited with the creation of mountains, volcanoes and coastlines. The Scandinavian sagas went even further. Early gods of the Nordic races were believed to have created the entire universe – earth, sky, seas and all the natural forces.

Such myths, dominating the culture and waking lives of native people, must also effect the dreams that they experience during sleep. These dreams, according to Jung, come from the collective unconsciousness of shared experience and beliefs.

In explaining the unconscious, Jung attempts to personify it as a being. 'He would have lived countless times over the life of the individual, of the family, tribe and people, and he would present the living sense of growth, flowering and decay.'

Dreams are one thing which we have in common with every society in the world.

Action Dreams Around the World

Dreams can have an effect of startling reality, sometimes remaining with us for most of the following day, or even for several days. Members of some African and Indian tribes take the reality factor very seriously. One report tells of a Paraguayan Indian who dreamt that a missionary shot at him. He then attempted to kill the missionary.

Jesuit priests in the 18th century reported that among Iroquois Indians it was obligatory to carry out the action of a dream as soon as possible. One Indian was said to have dreamed that 10 of his friends dived into a hole in the ice of a lake, and came up through another hole. When the friends were told of the dream, they duly enacted their roles in it. Unfortunately, though, only nine of them actually succeeded.

Kurdish people who dreamed of something valuable were expected to take it, using force if necessary. While among some natives of Kamchatka in Russia, if a man dreamt of a girl's favour it was traditionally considered her duty to have sex with him.

African and Indian Tribes

Islamic dreams are concerned almost entirely with the acquisition of valuable worldly goods in praise of Allah.

In parts of Africa, dream life is considered almost as important as waking life, and it is believed that many dream activities really take place. An African tribesman waking with stiff arm muscles may well believe that he acquired them while wielding a club during a dream battle.

Identifying dreams with reality can be disconcerting. One Macusi Indian of Guyana is reported to have become enraged at the European leader of an expedition. The Indian dreamed that the European had made him haul a canoe up dangerous cataracts. He woke exhausted and refused to believe that the dream was not real.

Smohalla and The Dreamers

To the Native Americans, dreams played a special part in the education and initiation of young people. A rich dream life, narrated in vivid detail, would win respect for a boy and his wisdom would be esteemed as valuable to the tribe.

Some dreams, however, were brought about by other means than sleep. Late in the 18th century Smohalla, a North American prophet and preacher, founded a religious cult called The Dreamers. The cult took its name from the importance Smohalla placed on dreams sent to himself and his priests by God, directing them in the ways they should take in their daily lives. The dream ritual included the beating of drums, the ringing of bells and ecstatic dancing, all of which combined to bring on visions and exaltation.

Oriental, Hindu and Islamic Dreams

Oriental dream traditions are contemplative and philosophical, and the dreamer's state of mind is considered of greater importance than predictive powers in a dream. Chinese scholars, in common with many other cultures, believed that the spiritual soul was temporarily separated from the body while dreaming. Chinese sages, recognizing that there are different levels of consciousness, take account of the dreamer's horoscope and physical condition, and also the time of year that the dream occurs.

Hindu dream tradition stresses the importance of individual dream images, and relates them to the symbols associated with both gods and demons. The Hindu belief that symbols may be either universal or individual to the dreamer foreshadows Jung's theory of the 'collective unconscious'.

Islamic dreams are concerned almost entirely with the acquisition of valuable worldly goods in praise of Allah, or of such gifts being received from Allah as a reward for piety. Bad dreams, however, are considered to be sent by the devil and should not be divulged.

The Balinese demon, Bombu, popularly regarded as a guardian against evil.

Eighteenth century war chariot with attendant demons. Bangkok.

What is a Dream?

Most of us will have experienced some form of dreaming when first falling asleep.

According to Prospero's philosophy in *The Tempest*, human life is a moment of wakeful dreaming between two periods of endless sleep. A little later in the same century, the French philosopher Descartes wondered whether there could be anything more real than a dream. Even as he pondered this, seated at his fireside, he questioned whether he was really awake or dreaming!

Hamlet's much quoted, 'To sleep, perchance to dream,' refers, of course, to the sleep of death, and our concern here is not with death, but with the dreams in life.

Freud saw the dream as a façade behind which unconscious meanings were hidden, often in sexually symbolic forms, and Jung admitted, 'I do not know how dreams arise.'

While Jung was an admirer and sometime follower of Freud, this was not to say he always agreed with him. 'If we meditate on a dream sufficiently long and thoroughly,' he maintained, 'something almost always comes out of it.'

He also explained that, to him, dreams were a part of nature, 'harbouring no intention to deceive but expressing something as best it can, just as a plant grows or an animal seeks its food as best it can.'

When do we Dream?

Dreams may take place at any stage during sleep. Most of us will have experienced some form of dreaming when first falling asleep, or while dozing in a car or train. This is usually in the form of visual images that reflect our last waking thoughts, and seldom develops into any sort of on-going dream situation.

Sensations of falling are quite common as we drift into sleep. These are known as 'myclonic' or muscular jerks, in which the sleeper has a feeling of falling off a step or kerb. Sometimes such sensations will wake us up, and the expression 'nodding off' seems apt.

Significant or cognitive dreaming, however, is associated with the paradoxical stage of sleep, in which the eyes move rapidly about. These are the dreams of primary interest to psychoanalysts, and the type mainly dealt with by Jung and Freud.

Why do we Dream?

Jung believed that one thing dreams strive to do is to give dreamers a more acute sense of balance. Certainly this theory, of dreaming as a means of keeping our mental and emotional balance, is finding favour with researchers today.

Jung had differentiated between the 'great' dreams of the collective unconscious, and the 'little' dreams of personal experience. The 'great' dreams occur less frequently, usually only at important stages of our lives. The 'little' dreams, on the other hand, use symbols from our daily life and are concerned with everyday matters.

Children have their own ideas as to why we dream. So that 'we know how to do things,' (small boy) or, 'for our brains to switch off and have a rest,' (small girl). Or, from an older girl, 'to show us what we are like on the inside.' An intriguing thought and not, perhaps, far from the truth!

Drugs & Alcohol

Although many people are reluctant to drink coffee before retiring, research shows that caffeine seems to have little effect on our normal sleep patterns.

The effects of alcohol are variable. The short-term effect is to reduce the time spent in REM (rapid eye movement) sleep. Continued use, however, may cause a REM sleep rebound, with the occurrence of more vivid and unpleasant dreams.

Addictive drugs such as barbiturates, amphetamines and narcotics also appear to be REM sleep deprivers. The unpleasant dreams associated with REM sleep rebound could be why some people return to the use of these drugs.

Grecian demonic women sometimes regarded as the spirits of vengeance. They work by disturbing the minds of those they seek to destroy.

We are such stuff As dreams are made on; and our little life is rounded with a sleep.
William Shakespeare
The Tempest.

The Science of Dreams

I do not believe that I am dreaming, but I cannot prove that I am not!

Bertram Russell.

EEG, or electroencephalograph measurements, are used in laboratory research to assess the brain activity of male and female volunteers during sleep. The electroencephalograph, first used by Hans Berger in 1926, is an instrument that records the electrical activity of the brain by using electrodes attached to the scalp.

In the first, or 'alpha' stage of sleep, the muscles relax and the heartbeat slows down. Stage two sleep shows quick bursts of short-wave brain activity known as 'spindles'. In stage three, large slow brainwaves occur, the heart rate continues to slow and body temperature and blood pressure drops.

Stage four, or 'delta' sleep (so called because of the large delta brainwaves) finds the sleeper almost immobile and very difficult to rouse. Up to and including this stage, the volunteer is in NREM (non-rapid eye movement) sleep.

Paradoxical Sleep

The final stage is REM (rapid eye movement), dreaming, or paradoxical sleep. The term 'paradoxical' is used because the EEG recorded brainwaves are characteristic of attentiveness, but there is little or no reaction to the outside world.

REM sleep indicates that dreaming is taking place. The eyes flicker below closed lids as if the dreamer is watching a film. The body shows greater tension, oxygen consumption increases and the adrenal glands behave as if preparing for action. Yet – paradoxically – despite all this mental and physical activity, the sleeper is immobile and the muscles are limp.

It is this physical immobility in REM sleep that has given rise to one explanation for 'incubus' or suffocating nightmares, in which the dreamer experiences a sensation of being unable to move or call out.

The usual progression of sleep is for the NREM stages to last for about 70-90 minutes, followed by a REM stage lasting for about 10-20 minutes. The sequence is repeated throughout the night, with the REM period lengthening somewhat. Hence, our most vivid and important dreams usually occur in the morning, just before we wake up.

The Theory of Dreams

Freud introduced the term 'psychoanalysis' in 1896. He engaged in extensive self-analysis, which led him to the recognition of infantile sexuality and the Oedipus complex.

He suggested that dreams were an attempt to satisfy, during sleep, ambitions and objectives which the dreamer had been unable to fulfil in waking life. He believed that while we were dreaming, our unconscious mind revealed desires that we should find offensive if they surfaced when we were awake.

Modern psychiatrists, however, give far less importance to the wish-fulfilment aspect of dreams, and tend to consider them in relation to the patient's general state of mind.

From Heronymous Bosch, 'The Garden of Heavenly Delights'.

Modern Thinking

Jung was probably closer to modern thinking than Freud, with whom he had collaborated for some years. Jung believed that the first step in understanding a dream was to establish its content. This meant unravelling its network of relationships with the dreamer and his or her life, and discovering the significance of the various images it presented.

Freud and Jung disagreed as to what is meant by a symbol. Freud gave fixed meanings to all dream images – doors, knives, teeth, caves, steeples all represented sexual objects. But Jung's approach was more creative. He believed the same symbol could represent different things to different dreamers, and even to the same dreamer in different circumstances.

To Freud and other psychoanalysts, dreams tended to be treated as neurotic symptoms rather than normal experiences. Modern psychoanalysts still make extensive use of dream analysis, but use patients' dreams to explore their current preoccupations rather than accepting them as 'fixed' images.

One psychoanalyst who rejected the Freudian theory claimed that if we all dream, then dreams cannot be regarded as a neurotic symptom. Unless, of course, we are all neurotic.

J A Hobson, a modern sleep specialist, maintains that the understanding of dreams offers insight into mental illness, because every dream with its dissociated states is a little – but healthy – psychosis.

What Does Your Child Dream?

The dream child moving through a land of wonders wild and new.

Lewis Carroll, 1865.

Many people ask at what age a child starts to dream. Surprisingly, there is evidence to suggest that dreaming takes place in the womb, particularly during the last three months of pregnancy. A large amount of REM (rapid eye movement) sleep is required both before and after birth to stimulate the central nervous system, which helps prepare for later structural growth.

We can only hazard a guess as to what a baby dreams about, but children from about two years of age do talk about their dreams when woken from REM sleep. Toddlers dream very largely about their daily lives, their families and about animals. Many two and three year olds associate dreaming with going to bed, rather than with going to sleep.

Symbols in Children's Dreams

School seems to feature very little in children's dreams, but location plays an important part in their dream-life. A child living on a farm, for instance, may have a 'bad dream' about falling into a slurry pit. An inner city child, on the other hand, may be more likely to dream about robbers, or attackers breaking into the house.

The image of the house symbolizes a sense of self, and is a relevant and recurring symbol to children as well as to adults. Computers, as symbols, play an important part in the child's dream-world. Television is also significant, and is responsible for many disturbing dreams.

During illness, children frequently have colourful dreams of abstract patterns, 'blobs' or blotches – nearly always behaving erratically. But a fear of dying and dreams of death are even more disturbing to a sick child. Such dreams are far more common than one may suppose. Children do worry about death, and it is very important for them to be able to talk about it.

Does Your Pet Dream?

Dog owners can be in no doubt that their pets dream, or that dreaming affects their waking lives much as it does our own. Having twitched or barked for several minutes, on waking, dogs will often wag their tails cheerfully as if having just returned from an energetic walk. Or they may look thoroughly cowed, as if expecting a reprimand. One thing is certain, if dogs could talk they would tell us their dreams – probably at length.

Cats are by far the greatest dreamers, simply because they spend more time sleeping than other animals. There are three types of feline sleep, the brief nap, the longer light sleep and the deep sleep. During the period of deep REM sleep the cat's body relaxes so much it usually rolls over on to its side. This is the dreaming period, with frequent twitching and quivering of ears, paws and tail. It is easy to imagine at this stage that the cat may be experiencing dreams of hunting and chasing.

Modern laboratory tests show that rats, monkeys – and even mice – exhibit REM sleep patterns. So while your cat is dreaming of the mouse that got away, that same mouse could be having a nightmare about the cat that almost caught it!

Light Sleepers

Horses certainly dream, and they can experience short-wave sleep (SWS) and dreams while standing up. Such dreams not infrequently occur when they are travelling in horse boxes. Rapid eye movement (REM) sleep and dreaming is also very important to horses, but they only experience this when lying flat on their sides.

Sheep, goats and cows are now thought to accomplish some sort of sleep, and some sort of dreaming, while chewing the cud with their eyes open.

Birds also dream for short periods. Even the owl dreams, although it is incapable of experiencing REM sleep because its tubular eyes are permanently fixed in their sockets.

The Dream Workshop

Awake and tell thy dream.
William Shakespeare,
Pericles.

*I*n our dreams we are, in a sense, talking to ourselves. The conversations we have, however, are more meaningful than the rather trivial 'thought-talk' in which we often indulge while carrying out boring tasks. When we dream it is our unconscious doing the talking, and listening to it could be more beneficial than we realize.

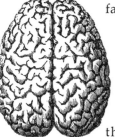

Why is it that some people are unable to recall their dreams? Psychological tests suggest that people who tend to avoid facing anxieties in daily life may show a reluctance to remember their dreams.

It would seem that non-recallers are often more controlled and conformist than those who do recall dreams. If your recall is poor and you accept that dreams can be of practical help to you, that fact alone may be a valuable first step on the path to memory improvement.

A much better rate of recall was shown by laboratory volunteers asked to remember their dreams, than by those not instructed to do so. It would seem, then, that it is possible to activate our recall mechanism if we are sufficiently motivated. And in this state of mind we are ready to embark upon dream exercises that should be both pleasurable and rewarding.

Improving Creativity – A Quiet Awakening

There are several methods for starting along the creative path of dream memory that Freud called the 'royal road to the unconscious mind.'

People awakened during REM sleep always seem to recall dreams. So setting an alarm clock at 90 minute intervals throughout the night and writing down at once what was in the mind before waking, could be effective. However, it is hardly likely to find favour with sleeping partners!

A more pleasurable method is to lie very quietly on waking, without moving and with the mind completely relaxed. Then, say to yourself that you remember a dream you had last night. Avoid telling yourself that you *must* remember as this can be inhibiting, and fear and inhibition are sworn enemies of dream recall. We are inhibited because we are afraid of what the dream is really trying to tell us, and so we conveniently forget it.

The Dream Diary

Have a notepad beside your bed and jot down anything you remember. Later, you can enter this in a dream diary in greater detail. Your dream diary should be special – it doesn't matter what sort of book you use – and kept solely for that purpose. It is a good idea to print DREAM DIARY in large letters on the front, you may then find that just opening the book is enough to trigger dream memories.

If you find writing difficult or inhibiting, try drawing pictures of what you remember. Draw any dream image that comes into your mind and almost certainly others will follow. Artistic ability, or lack of it, is quite unimportant.

If these methods do not work for you, try another. Get up earlier than usual, sit quietly and just write anything that comes into your head. Authors often do this to get over 'writer's block'. At first you may find yourself writing nonsense or recounting the previous day's happenings. But sooner or later, dream elements will probably appear in your jottings.

Group sessions are also used to overcome 'writer's block', and discussion can be just as helpful for dream recall. Writers may compose a group story, with each participant throwing in a phrase or image. Often, many of these images are dream memories, whether realized or not. You may find it helpful to discuss your dreams with like-minded friends.

There is no doubt that our dreams can help us to be more creative. Remember that creativity is not the prerogative of artists and poets. Running a house, or organizing a filing system can be just as creative in its own way.

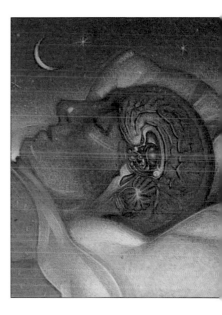

Dreams are faithful interpreters of our inclinations; but there is art required to sort and understand them.
Montaigne 1580.

Problem Solving

It is not uncommon for problems to be resolved – or seem to be resolved – while we sleep. Some part of the mind seems to continue working on the problem during the night, and in the morning we may find that we have a solution. Occasionally, the answer to a problem comes through a dream.

Elias Howe, American inventor of the sewing machine, was beset by a major problem in his design. He was unable to find a location for the eye of the needle. One night he dreamt that he was being led to his execution, and observed that the guards surrounding him all carried spears that were pierced near the head. Howe realized at once that this was the solution to his problem and, on waking, went straight to his workshop. That same morning, the first sewing machine was well on the way to completion.

Dream Messages

We should try to think of our dreams as friendly messengers, even if what they tell us is not always pleasant. Shakespeare's Cleopatra struck down the messenger who brought her news of Antony's marriage to Octavia. But, of course, the messenger was not to blame. Neither is a dream messenger to blame for a bad dream experience. The cause will be evident only if we face it and search for its meaning.

If we learn to read the signs, a voyage of discovery into our dream life can be exciting and enjoyable. It can also tell us a great deal about ourselves and what 'makes us tick'. We can discover how our unconscious can comment on our problems and help to resolve some of the complexities of waking life.

We should not, however, be over confident that our 'unconscious knows best'. As Jung pointed out, if this was the case there would be little virtue in being conscious.

Thou quiet soul,
sleep thou a
quiet sleep;
Dream of success
and victory.
William Shakespeare,
King Richard III.

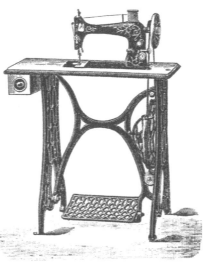

Lucid Dreaming

Lucid dream research is still young, and much is yet to be discovered. Lucid dreamers are aware that they are dreaming, and the dreams experienced in this state are sometimes remembered with unusual precision.

Flying dreams can be lucid. The dreamer knows it is possible to 'take off' from roof or cliff-top 'because it is a dream', and the ensuing sensation may be exhilarating.

Recent research by an American scientist suggests that lucid dreamers suffer less from neurosis and depression. Yet Wagner suffered excessively from both these maladies, and he was a lucid dreamer. In one dream (recorded by his wife) he found himself in a hall full of classical busts which could speak. Attracted to a particular female bust, he said to himself 'I do not wish to dream that I kissed her, because it is not good to kiss dead people in your dreams.'

Our truest life is when we are in dreams awake.
H. D. Thoreau, 1849.

For ne'er was a dream So like a wakening.
William Shakespeare,
The Winter's Tale.

A Fuller Awakening

Lucid dreams have been experimentally induced in sleep laboratories and seem to occur only during REM sleep. They are not common, and many people never experience them at all.

Stephen LaBerge, founder of the *Lucidity Institute of California* believes it is possible to teach lucid dreaming, and that it prepares dreamers for a 'fuller awakening' (see glossary). Some researchers claim that lucid dreams provide the dreamer with a better understanding of a situation, because characters can be questioned and symbols examined.

One young boy tells of his own method of dealing with unpleasant dreams. 'I decide I don't want to dream any more, so I open my eyes very wide and wake up!'

Controlled lucid dreaming may enable us to change the course of a bad dream, or invoke delightful images. But if our dreams are talking to us, should we really be telling them what to say?

The Dream Library

The dream's here still. Even when I wake it is without me, as within me.
William Shakespeare, *Cymbeline.*

We usually know when we've had an important dream by its vividness, and the way it 'stays with us' on waking. Often, however, we can tell neither why the dream was important, nor its particular significance to us personally.

An understanding of the themes and types of dreams that occur most frequently is a step toward successful interpretation. But it is only the first step. Apart from the 'Great' dreams of mythology, most dreams are personal and the messages they contain are addressed to us, the dreamer, and to no one else.

Dreams of disasters that effect large numbers of people can be predictive, but more often reveal personal anxieties. To dream of an earthquake could indicate feelings of insecurity in waking life. Buildings crashing down may suggest a collapse of personal ambitions or material aims – and so on.

However, this is not to say that we should scoff at warnings. If you dreamt that a falling slate hit you on the head as you left your house, it would certainly be an idea to examine the roof. In dreams such as these our unconscious has often picked up clues that our conscious mind may have missed.

Warning Dreams

Cats, who so often avoid disaster, are sometimes credited with uncanny powers of premonition. Perhaps it is because they have a constant awareness of those unconscious warnings that are revealed to us in dreams.

Warning dreams have always been with us. They appear in history and literature, in memoirs and in modern journalism. In *Richard III*, Clarence's vividly related dream of being drowned by his brother was a warning, but did nothing to prevent his subsequent murder.

President Abraham Lincoln dreamt that he entered a room in the White House and was confronted by a coffin, draped in black for a lying in state. 'Who is dead?' he asked the guard on duty. 'The president,' the man replied. Lincoln is reputed to have discussed this dream with several people just before he was assassinated.

A few years ago in Britain, a lorry driver recounted a dream to his wife. She reports he had dreamt of a motorway accident in which he killed a child. Disturbed by the dream, he decided not to drive that day and his friend took the wheel.

In torrential rain, the lorry ploughed into the back of a pick-up truck that had broken down. The lorry driver was hurled through the windscreen from the passenger seat of the lorry, and killed. No child was involved, but the lorry driver seems to have dreamt of his own death.

Alarm or Preparation?

Warning dreams are always particularly vivid. Sometimes they take the form of alarms that it may, or may not be possible to heed. At other times they seem to be preparing the dreamer for what will happen.

During the war, in England, a laboratory chemist was making up smoke bombs for use in Home Guard exercises One of the bombs combusted spontaneously and the man was badly burnt. When he regained consciousness in hospital his wife was at his bedside, and he marvelled at her composure. Some time later she told him she had dreamed of the accident several months before it happened, and knew what to expect.

Avoiding action can sometimes be taken if the warning dream is practical. The Duke of Portland, who helped to organize the coronation of King Edward VII, dreamt that the king's coach stuck while passing through an arch on the way to Westminster Abbey.

The arch was duly measured and was found to be almost two feet too low to allow the coach to pass through. The dream was heeded and action was taken – and the embarrassment of a topless royal coach was averted.

I did dream to-night The Duke was dumb and could not speak a word.
William Shakespeare,
Henry VI, Part two.

Your Dream Body

What a piece of work is a man.
William Shakespeare,
Hamlet.

In sickness, the ancient Greeks and Romans would sleep in the temple of a god to receive dream information about a remedy. This was known as 'dream incubation' and was widely practised.

Hippocrates (born c. 460BC), after whom the Hippocratic oath was named, believed that dreams revealed the unseen workings of both body and soul. Even today, with the outstanding advances in medical science, dreams still reveal a great deal about our body and our state of health.

Freud described a number of dream images that represented the body. The favourite image was a house, with the upper part representing the upper body of the dreamer, and so forth. He gave one example of a headache being indicated in a dream by a ceiling crawling with disgusting insects and 'toad-like spiders'.

Freud believed it could sometimes take a whole row of houses to represent a single organ, such as the intestine. But even more intriguing was his symbolism for 'dreams with a dental stimulus'. He described an 'entrance hall with a high vaulted roof' as corresponding to the inside of the mouth, with a staircase to the 'descent from the throat to the oesophagus' (gullet).

A Blazing Furnace

House symbolism apart, Freud suggested the heart may be represented by hollow boxes or baskets, the bladder by round, bag-shaped objects and the lungs by a blazing furnace 'with flames roaring with a sound like the passage of air.'

Freud also drew attention to the fact that Aristotle (b.384BC) considered it quite possible that the beginnings of illnesses might make themselves felt in dreams, before anything could be noticed of them in waking life. Neither did medical writers of Freud's time dispute the significance of dreams as warnings of illness.

Health Warnings

If we dream about a particular area of our body, it could mean that it needs some attention. Sometimes, in sleep we seem to be given psychological and physiological signals that are not always evident to a doctor.

Migraine may start in childhood and dreams can warn parents of impending attacks. Aggression is frequently experienced in pre-migraine dreams, but even more common are situations of complete terror. To detect the emergence of pre-migraine dream patterns, it is important to listen regularly to the child's dreams.

Disturbing dreams also play an important part in night-time asthma attacks in children. If a child has had a stressful day, this is likely to be reflected in his or her dreams. The dreams may then bring on an attack of asthma.

Sleep-Walking

Night activity, such as sleep-walking, is not uncommon in children. Providing the child can come to no physical harm there is seldom any need for medical attention. Sleep-walking in adults can be more serious, and may follow a particularly distressing experience.

Sleep activity, such as miming washing the hands or attempting to carry out a task, is also a sign of mental disturbance. Lady Macbeth's sleep-walking scene, in which she tries repeatedly to cleanse the blood from her hands, typifies such an action following trauma – in this case, of course, of her own making.

People who dream lucidly and have frequent dream recall may also have out-of-body (OOB) experiences. This is when the world is perceived from outside the physical body. Dreamers have occasionally reported difficulty in getting back into their bodies, or of feeling disinclined to do so.

Television viewers are probably aware that astral travel or OOB experiences have been reported by those awake, or under anaesthetic as well as during dreams.

Out-of-body (OOB) experiences are when the world is perceived from outside the physical body.

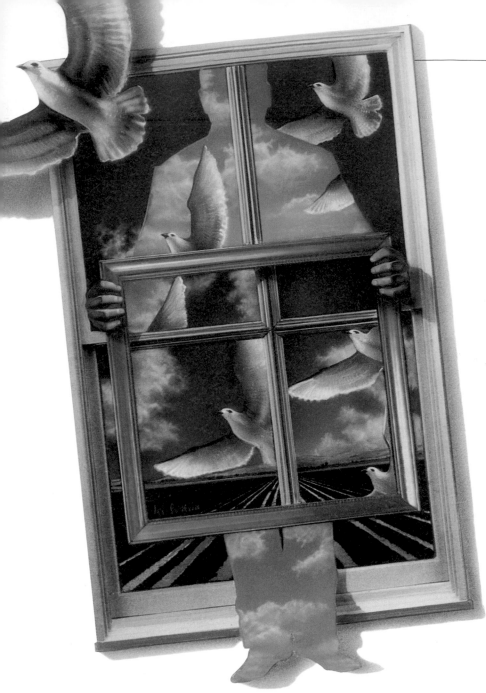

However, we do not always appreciate the necessity of such dreams, and fail to receive the messages that they are trying to convey to us. In this case they are often repeated as recurring dreams until we do take notice of them, and the object of their continued recurrence is to tell us something important about ourselves.

Reading the Signs

Recurring dreams often reflect problems that something in our waking life has 'triggered' in our unconscious mind. When we start to read the signs correctly, the dream can tell us what stage we have reached in resolving the problem, or if we have made any progress at all.

It is important to enter recurring dreams in the Dream Diary with particular care. Record each detail every time you have the dream, paying special attention to any subtle variations in it. If carefully observed, these details will help you to understand a little more about the dream each time it occurs.

Recurring dreams are sometimes disturbing, and head-on confrontation is the only way to deal with them. So, if a dream is trying to tell you something about yourself that you don't want to hear, it is probably a good time to be listening!

*In the course of
my life I have
often had the same
dream.*
Plato, 380BC

Recurring Dreams

Why, if dreaming is a necessary part of our emotional development, are so many of our dreams forgotten? Some theorists maintain it is because forgetting is also a necessary part of the process.

According to these theorists, one of the functions of REM sleep is to erase memories that have become redundant or 'parasitic', because they have no place in our present view of the world. Such memories are wiped from our mind in sleep, rather as an unwanted document is 'deleted' from a computer. Other, necessary, dreams are 'saved' and therefore remembered.

Deep-Rooted Anxiety

Some theorists maintain that recurring dreams are remembered because they usually wake us up. This is certainly true of the genuine nightmare, in which there is no visual presence, but an overwhelming sensation of suffocation and immobility.

Such dreams sometimes indicate deep-rooted anxiety, or sexual repression and dealing with them is important, especially if they occur frequently.

Write the experience in your Dream Diary and follow it immediately with a description – or drawing – of what you imagine the terrifying presence would have looked like if it had materialized. By facing your fears in this way you are taking the first steps on the road to understanding them.

Secrets from Outer Space

Freud claimed that recurrent dreams were first dreamt in childhood, and then constantly reappeared from time to time in adult sleep. Spacemen, nuclear war and even the ozone layer are recurring images in the dreams of today's children. When such images are carried forward to adulthood, however, they usually represent something more complex.

Sarah, an artist, has recurring dreams about UFOs. In her dream, she is the only one on earth to know that they have landed, and this secret knowledge is probably more significant than the image (UFOs) that engenders it.

Dreams that we are in possession of some special secret are not uncommon, but it is our reaction to the possession of the secret that is important. If we feel anxious or guilty, then perhaps we are being too secretive about a waking situation.

Sometimes, recurring dreams can be telling us several things at the same time. Robert frequently dreams that he switches on the lights in the house and they fail to work. The switches could represent a dream sex pun, (is Robert 'switched on'?) but failing lights may indicate a longing for greater spiritual illumination.

When all is said, melancholy is the mother of dreams, and of all terrors of the night whatsoever.

Thomas Nash, *The Terrors of the Night*, 1594

Freud suggested that a mental device which he called the 'censor' attempts to translate dream material into symbolic forms that appear less offensive to the conscious mind. In this way the dreamer's sleep is preserved.

Freud's theory presumes some sort of competition between the unconscious mind (which he termed the 'id') and the conscious mind, (the 'ego'). However, later research suggests that rather than being in competition, the id and the ego are more likely to coexist as partners.

The 'True Dream' Disguised

Wish-fulfilment implies pleasure, and it was therefore argued that unpleasant or anxiety dreams could hardly be wish-fulfilling. Freud maintained that the 'true dream' was frequently disguised in the symbolic manner already explained, and must therefore be 'decoded' for the connotation to be found.

Freud was once giving a course of lectures on dreams with unwished for contents which were, nevertheless, wish-fulfilment dreams. He claimed that a young physician attending the lectures unconsciously adapted this 'theme' into a dream of his own.

The day before, the young physician had sent in his income-tax return, which he had filled in with perfect honesty, as he had very little to declare. He then dreamt that an acquaintance came to him from a meeting with the tax commissioners and informed him that, while no objections had been raised to any of the other tax returns, general suspicion had been aroused by his and a heavy fine had been imposed upon him.

Freud interpreted this dream as a poorly disguised fulfilment of the young physician's wish to be known as a doctor with a large income.

Wish-Fulfilment Dreams

Freud believed that most dreams are 'wish-fulfilments', or expressions of repressed desires that gain access to our unconscious mind while we sleep. But many of these desires are primitive, and being unacceptable to our conscious mind would be expected to wake us up.

Oh! that my young life were a lasting dream!

Edgar Allen Poe,

Dreams 1827

Returning to the Past

Wish-fulfilment dreams of returning to places associated with the past are common. We may dream of going back to school or college, or of returning to a house in which we used to live. Such dreams hint that there may be a strong desire to live life again as we did once before. They could also indicate a reluctance to face changes.

Some dreams are quite straightforward and no decoding is required. Winning the pools, or the lottery, are obvious wish-fulfilment dreams. And people who have given up smoking frequently dream of enjoying a dream cigarette.

Bereavement may trigger deeper wish-fulfilment dreams. If the person who has died was very close to us, dreaming about them could be an important part of the healing process of grieving.

A Dream Discovery

Other dreams can be rather more obscure. Jean was the passive partner in her marriage and her husband made all the decisions, including furnishing and decorating the house. One night Jean dreamt that she discovered an orange hat in a department store. She knew it wouldn't suit her, but felt so elated by her discovery that she simply had to buy it.

Sometime afterwards, Jean bought an orange table-cloth and window blind for the kitchen dining area. It was not until much later, during discussion, that she associated this first step toward independence with her hat dream.

Rena started an affair with a man she had known for some time. She said she had felt no physical attraction toward him until she dreamt one night that they were having sex together. After that the attraction was undeniable and, fortunately, mutual. Rena thought her dream was premonitory, but it was more likely to have been pure wish-fulfilment – her unconscious picking up clues of sexual attraction that her conscious mind had hitherto concealed from her.

I had a dream – and there mine eyes did see The shadows of past deeds like present things. . .

Elizabeth Barrett Browning

Sexual Dreams

Freud has been criticized for his insistence that certain dream symbols always mean the same thing. A snake, for instance, is always a phallic symbol according to Freud. He also maintains that 'all weapons and tools are used as symbols for the male organ', while shafts, passages and other openings are consistently represented as vaginal symbols.

Freud himself denies that he asserts that all dreams require sexual interpretation. Nevertheless, he does attach much weight to the sexual interpretation of seemingly innocuous objects.

However, as most analysts agree that sexual symbols are often present in dreams, it is not impossible that almost any symbol we encounter could be telling us something about our sex-life. Therefore, it is very important to examine our attitude to sex and to recognize the need for sexual fulfilment. At the same time, we should also be on guard against over-emphasizing the sexual theme in dreams.

The Naked Truth

Dreaming of nudity is often associated with sexuality. In some cases this may be true, but as always the dreamer's reaction to the situation is important. If you are naked among people who are regarding you with amazement or disgust, it could mean that you need to relax more with your partner, or to try to be less self-critical.

On the other hand, you should always be aware to the possibility of dream puns. Nakedness could suggest personal integrity, revealing the 'bare facts' or the 'naked truth'. If you are being flamboyant about your nakedness, playing the part of a stripper, for example, then you may have a desire to shock people.

Of course, the dream could be a reaction to what you feel is a restrictingly conventional waking life, either at home or in the office. Diligent recording and honest assessment are needed to 'uncover' the truth about any dream – sexual or otherwise.

The 'Pleasure Principle'

Freud refers to a 'primary' type of thinking in the unconscious mind as the 'pleasure principle', whereby the gratification of infantile sexual desires is achieved. He believed sexual imagery to be the driving force of dream symbolism. Jung – who believed that even explicit sexual themes could symbolize the higher creative process – was more open minded about symbolism.

Theorists have claimed that sexual dreams are simply the result of sexual tension demanding an outlet. Yet men so badly injured that they are incapable of any sexual feelings still report having such dreams.

Sexual dreams are common to us all, and if the dream is enjoyable there is no cause for concern. When the sexual content is unduly aggressive or distasteful, however, the dream may be revealing something about our sexuality that we should note with care. Dreams with disguised sexual content also require careful study.

Alison's Dream

Puns occur frequently in dreams. They can be openly amusing or, as we have seen, presented obscurely in some other form.

Alison dreamt that she was working in the garden at the side of the house. Suddenly, the downpipe came away from the gutter and she was drenched by a gush of water. Unperturbed by her soaking, she said to herself, 'I suppose this is what you'd call a wet dream!' and was sufficiently amused by the 'pun' to wake up chuckling.

Water gushing from a tap or faucet is often a symbol of ejaculation, representing the sexual act. Alison's 'wetting' may have been more than an obvious pun and signalled something important about her sexuality.

The pipe 'came away' from its normal position, perhaps indicating something wrong in her sex-life. She may have felt that a desire to be more sexually assertive or 'masculine' was out of place.

Anxiety Dreams

Many of our dream sequences and symbols represent anxiety in one form or another. And, as we know, excessive anxiety can sometimes make it difficult to get to sleep in the first place.

At one time there was an apprehension about sleep itself, largely caused by the sleeper's physical vulnerability to enemies.

The vampire legend gained its power because of the helplessness of the sleeping victim.

Victims of nightmares may still share that apprehension. The recurring nightmare strongly indicates a deep-seated anxiety or repression. If we don't heed it, and work to interpret it, we may be leaving the window open to our own particular 'vampire'.

A Never-Ending Task

Anxiety dreams are not always nightmares, but they are recognizable by an emotional energy that is far from pleasant. Typical 'sensations' are those of trying to cope with several tasks at the same time, or attempting to complete a single, never-ending task.

If social inadequacy is the cause of anxiety, this may be reflected in dreams in which we are being painfully humiliated in public.

Dreams in which we 'worry' about something are very common. The worry itself may seem trivial compared to our waking problems, or seem to have little to do with them. However, if anxiety is expressed in a dream, it will be playing some part in our waking life.

It is important to examine such dreams closely. In this way we may discover areas in our life about which we are uncertain – and to which we have never given enough thought. Freud thought that anxiety dreams were the result of a wish to repress desires or emotions that were usually of a sexual origin.

This may be so, or the unconscious doubts and fears may reflect more mundane problems. In either case, it is essential to find the source of the anxiety in our waking life.

. . . in children's chase dreams, computers may give chase, or pull the child inside through the visual screen.

Chase Dreams

A very common anxiety dream is – like Alice with the Red Queen – trying to run and finding one's feet rooted to the spot.

Dreams of being pursued are also common, and can be very frightening. The pursuer may be an unseen presence, an animal, a person, or a terrifying 'thing'. There seems, in fact, no limit as to what, or who, might give chase to us in our dreams.

The chase dream usually indicates that something – or some problem – in our unconscious is trying hard to gain access to our conscious mind. It is important that we help the process by making careful notes of every aspect of the dream.

What form did our pursuer take? If it was an animal, what is our waking reaction to that particular animal – liking, tolerance, hate, fear? Was our pursuer gaining on us, or did we out-distance 'it'?

If we were able to turn and face the pursuer, we will have taken a big step toward overcoming our fear.

Pursued by a Washing Machine

Washing machines, and even toilets 'opening and closing and eating people up' have been reported in children's chase dreams. Computers may give chase, or pull the child inside through the visual screen. Children often dream that they are being chased by inanimate objects as well as by people, monsters and fierce animals.

Adult anxiety dreams are frequently characterized by actions such as crawling through a narrow tunnel (believed to represent birth anxiety), wading through cloying mud, or watching cherished possessions being destroyed.

A typical anxiety dream is one in which the dreamer's teeth are falling out. This is reported more commonly in women's dreams, and is interpreted as reflecting feelings of insecurity about looks and separation – 'falling out' with friends or relatives. Of course, it could simply suggest that a visit to the dentist is overdue!

Dreams of Success and Failure

Success and failure are two of our most common preoccupations, so it is hardly surprising that they are frequently presented in our dreams. Whatever our anxieties, in our heart of hearts we know that failure can be overcome. And, if we are not careful, we know that success can be short-lived.

. . . the dream must be studied carefully before we can interpret it.

This is reflected in mythology by the fate that befell Bellerophon, a Greek warrior who achieved many successes and victories with the aid of the winged horse, Pegasus. However, when he attempted to ride Pegasus to heaven, the horse threw him and Bellerophon ended his life as a lonely outcast.

Success in a dream may be represented by the favourable completion of a transaction, possibly accompanied by a feeling of elation. Jumping over a hurdle, or fence, may suggest overcoming an obstacle in waking life, while winning a race indicates a recognition of the dreamer's potential.

Failure may be presented by communication breakdowns, such as not being able to make oneself heard on the telephone, which suggest feelings of inadequacy.

Shared Anxiety Dreams

Most of us worry about failure in our own particular environment, or working life, and people sharing the same occupations frequently experience very similar anxiety dreams.

Nearly every actor will admit that he – or she – has recurring dreams about forgetting lines, not having learnt a part, or being on stage in the wrong play altogether. Climbers not infrequently have frightening dreams of 'exposure' on a sheer rock-face, and fighter pilots relate sharing the same, or very similar dreams about crashing their aircraft.

The Roman poet and philosopher Lucretius (b.98BC) seemed to sum it up, '. . . whatever be the pursuit to which one clings with devotion, whatever the things on which we have been occupied much in the past . . . it is generally the same things that we seem to encounter in dreams.'

Irma's Dream

Freud asserts that in every dream it is possible to find a point of contact with the experiences of the previous day. This is not to say, of course, that the 'point of contact' is immediately recognizable. More often than not it is represented symbolically, and the dream must be studied carefully before we can interpret it.

Freud cites his own dream of 'Irma' as an example of the representation of a recent experience, and in this case the point of contact is instantly apparent.

Irma was Freud's patient, whom he was treating for hysteria, and who annoyed him by disobeying his instructions. He dreamed that he found her to have an infection similar to diphtheria and had to conclude that he had diagnosed and treated her wrongly. The reasons he then gave himself to prove he was not at fault were, he admitted, contradictory.

'Irma's Dream' seems to fall into the 'occupational anxiety' category, and it would not be unreasonable to suppose that other psychoanalysts may have experienced similar dreams.

. . . in every dream it is possible to find a point of contact with the experiences of the previous day.

The 'Great' Dream of Truk

Shared dreams are common to every part of the world. On the Pacific island of Truk, for example, the natives share the same dream of falling out of coconut trees.

The 'Great Dream of Truk', as it is called, has many points of comparison with Jung's 'Great' dreams of mythology. However, as the islanders probably depend on coconut gathering for at least part of their livelihood, we shall conveniently class· it as an occupational anxiety dream!

Jung mentions yet another form of dream sharing. He notes that close friends or members of the same family – particularly husbands and wives or parents and children – will have the same dream without previously having told it to each other.

Dreams of Flying and Falling

Do you recognize the view? Does the landscape below mean something to you in waking life?

Flying and falling dreams could well be included among Jung's 'Great' dreams, as they are so deeply rooted in literature and mythology.

One such legend tells of Daedalus, a Greek craftsman and inventor, who made wings out of wax and feathers for himself and his son, Icarus. However, Icarus flew too near the sun, the wax from his wings melted and he fell into the sea and drowned.

Freud classifies flying and falling dreams as being 'typical', because they 'occur in large numbers of people and with very similar content.' He also includes teeth falling out and the embarrassment of being naked, or insufficiently clothed, among such dreams.

Down, down, down. Would the fall never come to an end?
Lewis Carroll, *Alice's Adventures in Wonderland.*

Freud puts forward a colleague's theory as to the tactile reasons for flying and falling dreams. Flying, he quotes as being attributed to the physical sensations from the rise and fall of the lungs during sleep.

Falling from a height, on the other hand, is attributed to involuntary sleep movements of the body, such as a flexed knee being suddenly extended.

Childhood Games

Freud, however, rejected these theories. He had no experience of flying dreams himself, but concluded that they related to memories of childhood games of swinging, or being playfully thrown into the air by adults. He claimed that such games of movement could give rise to sexual feelings, and that these sensations are recalled in dreams of flying.

Sex is not the only interpretation that other researchers have advanced for flying dreams. But it is true that the feeling of elation, sometimes experienced during such dreams, could be likened to pleasurable sex.

Freud admits being unable to produce any complete explanation for flying or falling dreams. He suggests that falling dreams may indicate anxiety, and that for women they are a symbolic representation of a surrender to temptation. He cites the expression, current in his time, of 'the fallen woman'.

Freedom in Flight

Flying dreams are very rarely unpleasant, and seldom related to falling dreams. Usually, if the dreamer 'lands' after a flight, it is by means of a gentle floating down to earth. The sense of freedom engendered by flying dreams may open the dreamer's imagination to infinite possibilities. Such dreams are often associated with ambition, and in interpreting them it is important to note how the flight was achieved.

If 'taking off' was difficult, it may suggest problems relating to waking ambitions or desires. Perhaps you should examine these more carefully and redefine your direction. You may be wasting energy unnecessarily.

If you fly effortlessly and achieve height easily, perhaps you are really 'flying high' due to some waking achievement. Soaring above the trees can be exhilarating.

Do you recognize the view? Does the landscape below mean something to you in waking life? You may have found yourself at the top of a high building and simply stepped off and taken flight.

If you reached the top of the building effortlessly it suggests self-confidence. Climbing up stairs and passages may have sexual connotations.

Soft Landings

Some people believe that if you actually land in a falling dream, you will die. This is quite untrue. Many dreamers experience a 'landing' and it is usually soft and painless.

Occasionally, one may dream of being hurt in the fall, although never fatally. If this happens to you, it may be necessary to examine your waking life carefully. Are you, perhaps, pushing yourself 'over the edge', or heading for a situation where an unpleasant fall is inevitable?

Falling dreams may suggest feelings of being out of control, or they may indicate the need to 'let go'. On the other hand, they may simply reflect a physical fear of falling.

The sense of freedom engendered by flying dreams may open the dreamer's imagination to infinite possibilities.

Just for You

The waking have one world in common; sleepers have each a private world of their own.

Heraclitus, 55BC

Most of our dreams are personal. Jung's 'Great' dreams, and genuine precognitive and warning dreams have a much wider implication, of course. But the majority of our dreams are individual and intimate, and it is these elements that we must be aware of when we search for the meanings.

In Jean's 'hat' dream, for example (see page 43), the colour orange obviously related to her need to be bolder, and to show more confidence. Yet she was unaware of this until much later, although she actually used the colour in making her first independent decisions in waking life. Jean's dream was pleasant, and its realization opened up the possibilities for personality development and a more fulfilling future.

Far more frequently our dream symbols – be they colours, objects or incidents – require us to look to the past, or deep within our own consciousness. This is never easy and may not be pleasant – sometimes, in fact, it takes quite a lot of courage. However, the personal benefits are well worth while.

Sit down quietly with your Dream Diary and say to yourself, 'I don't have to tell anyone about this dream unless I want to. But I do need to know what it's trying to tell me!'

Breaking the Code

You may be wondering how you can interpret your dreams correctly if you can never be sure what the images, or symbols represent for you, personally.

Dream symbols are often deliberate deceivers, they 'code' the messages for us, because otherwise we could find them unacceptable. Once we recognize this, breaking the code becomes that much easier.

Jung uses the example of a deal (or pine) table to illustrate the obscurity of dream imagery. He maintains that if someone dreams of a 'deal table' it is not enough for the dreamer to associate it with a desk (or dressing table, etc) not made of deal.

'Suppose that nothing more occurs to the dreamer, this blocking has an objective meaning, for it indicates that a particular darkness reigns in the immediate neighbourhood of the dream image, and that is suspicious.' Jung would expect the dreamer to have many associations to a deal table, and the fact that there are none he finds significant.

'In such cases I keep on returning to the image, and I usually say . . . "Suppose I had no idea what the words 'deal table' mean. Describe the object and give me its history in such a way that I cannot fail to understand what sort of thing it is." In this way we manage to establish almost the whole context of the dream image. When we have done this

for all the images in the dream we are ready for the venture of interpretation.'

Simon's Dream

Simon dreamt that he would climb the steps to the top of a tower-like building at night, wearing a black cloak, and then fly effortlessly wherever he chose. One night, he looked down to see a crowd of people staring up at him expectantly. He knew immediately that he could no longer fly, but he had to jump because the people below expected it.

Simon and his wife belonged to a writers' group, and Simon interpreted his dream as a new writer's doubt of the market value of his work. His interpretation was false, however. He was having an affair with a young married woman in the group, and his dream reflected his anxiety that he would be 'discovered'.

The tower represented Simon himself, and climbing up steps symbolized the sexual act. Night flying reflected the pleasures of clandestine sex with his mistress, while wearing a black cloak suggested that Simon was also carrying a 'burden' of gloom, or guilt.

We oft forget our dreams so speedily; if we cannot catch them as they are passing out at the door, we may never set eyes on them again.
William Hazlitt, 1826

Themes & Meanings

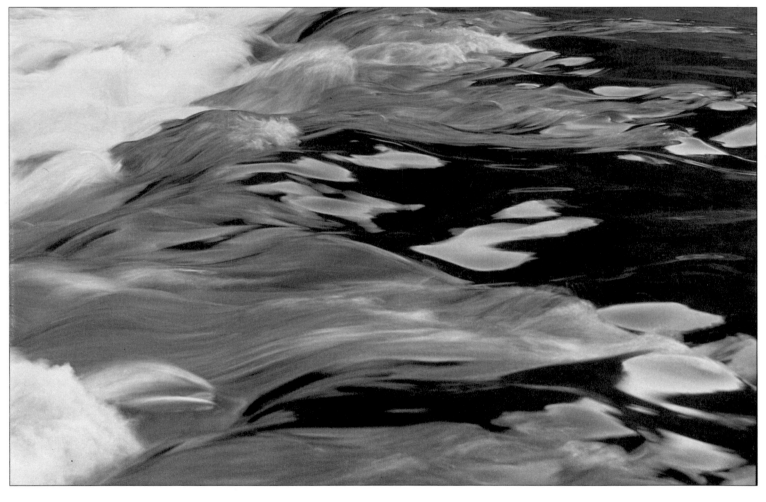

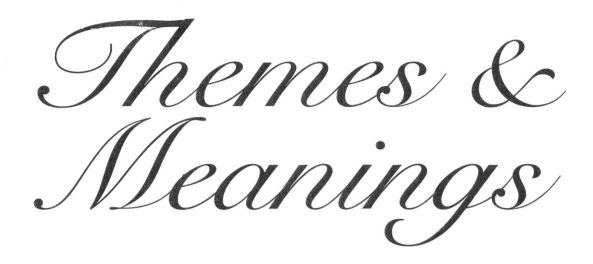

The following section enables you to look up various subjects and symbols that occur in your dreams, each under its own 'theme'. It is, of course, impossible to include everything that you are likely to dream about. However, if you use Themes and Meanings jointly with the Dream Workshop and the Dream Library, you will begin to have a comprehensive guide.

Themes

Think of Themes and Meanings as a mental location for your dreams, and go first to the place where they will most commonly be found. An aeroplane, for example, will be under the theme heading 'Transport', a table under 'Domestic', an elephant under 'Fish, Flesh and Fowl' – and so on. But remember, this is only the starting point.

You may ride your dream elephant past buildings and traffic ('Environment'), or it may fly with you over countryside ('Landscape'). You will now begin to question whether, in fact, your first dream symbol was the most important one after all!

In this way, you are exploring your dreams thoroughly. The theme section is cross-referenced to 'signpost' you on your journey, so use it together with your Dream Diary.

You will find that charting your dream life is both exciting and rewarding, and you will begin to discover the relevance of certain symbols for you, personally.

The Personal Interpretation

Having recalled our dream and then found a meaning for it in the themes and meanings section, we may feel we have accomplished a successful interpretation. In this case we are relying on our unconscious to be honest with us, and we could be sadly misled!

As Jung pointed out, '. . . the unconscious [mind] functions satisfactorily only when the conscious mind fulfils its task to the full.' There is much conscious work to be done before we can achieve a correct interpretation, and the importance of seeking out the 'personal connection' cannot be overstated.

Feathers, for instance, are generally considered a good omen in a dream. But if we have an allergy to them and can't bear them near us, then this dream will have quite a different interpretation.

It may be a health warning, for example, or a hint to keep away from something irritating or potentially harmful.

The unconscious is capable of all kinds of subterfuge.

Colin's Dream

Colin was made redundant and remained unemployed for a year. One night he dreamt that he was driving a Rolls Royce. Then, a few weeks later, he was offered a very good job which he accepted, albeit with some feelings of apprehension.

Before taking up his new position, Colin had another dream about the Rolls Royce. This time it was shabby and uncared for, and as he was driving down a hill the brakes failed and the vehicle careered on, out of control. At which point he woke up.

Consulting a dream dictionary, Colin discovered that failed brakes could mean that the dreamer should consider any new offer very carefully, as there may be hidden snags. Recalling his feelings of apprehension, he was inclined to turn the job down, and but for his wife's tearful remonstrating he may have done so.

Colin took the interpretation too literally, without relating the facts to himself. His apprehension was due to his own lack of confidence, which had been building up all the time he was out of work. It was this lack of confidence that had presented itself as a doubt about the integrity of the job offer.

The unconscious, as we have seen, is capable of all kinds of subterfuge. In this case it 'disguised' the fact that Colin's doubts were about himself, and related them to a different cause.

We are what we dream. Working to interpret our dreams correctly will almost certainly bring us to a fuller understanding of ourselves.

Activity

Decorating

What was being decorated, and who was doing the decorating? If you were the decorator, it could be a hint to 'put your house in order', or perhaps to look more closely at your personal image. If a room in the house was being decorated, what significance does that particular room have for you?

Digging

A dream that poses some questions for the dreamer. What were you digging for? What, if anything, did you find? The dream could suggest that you are getting to the root of a psychological problem, and that you are ready to 'uproot' it.

Eating

Eating dreams can be motivated by actual hunger, but often self-discipline is also involved. If you were 'gorging' on food, it could represent a hunger for affection or security. If you had to pay for the food you ate, it may suggest that you are attempting to 'buy' love or friendship.

Gambling

A dream of opposite meaning. So if you dreamt of winning a fortune, it could be a warning not to take risks. Very occasionally, people have dreamt of 'lucky numbers' or the name of a horse that wins a race. But remember, your unconscious is quite capable of playing tricks on you.

Games

According to Freud, most games have sexual connotations. Your opponent in a dream game could certainly be a partner, or your lover. But the game may suggest that there is an aspect of your own sexuality about which you are none too confident.

Abandon
(see THREAT, p91)
Floating
(see EMOTION & DESIRE, p72)
Ironing
(see DOMESTIC, p70)
Nagging
(see RELATIONSHIPS, p89)
Shooting
(see THREAT, page 93)

Jumping

The 'jump' sometimes experienced as we are falling asleep is muscular, and has no other significance. But if you dreamed that you were jumping over an obstacle, it could reflect waking ambitions or objectives. Whether you succeeded or not is obviously relevant. How and where did you land? Perhaps you are being cautioned to 'look before you leap'.

Learning

This dream could be pure wish-fulfilment. You may feel that you need more time to study, or that you are less educated than you would like to be. It may also imply that you should 'prepare yourself', mentally, in some way. Then again, perhaps the dream is suggesting that a period of self-exploration is required (see also 'School', AUTHORITY, page 62).

Party

If the party was frivolous, it may be a hint that you are not taking life seriously enough. If you were giving the party and it was difficult to organize, perhaps you are not feeling completely 'in control'. If no one came to your party, it could reflect fears of social inadequacy (see also 'Banquet', FOOD & DRINK, page 79).

Race

If you were taking part in the dream race, were you a winner or a loser? The results may reflect your progress in waking life. Perhaps you should also see GAMBLING.

Running

The dream may suggest that you are trying to escape from a psychological problem. If you were frightened, who – or what – was chasing you? (see page 47). Or perhaps you were running to reach a goal? If so, your success or failure could reflect your progress in a waking situation.

Sailing

If you were sailing on calm waters, the dream indicates financial success and optimism – everything is 'plain sailing', in fact. But if you were sailing on stormy waters, perhaps you should exercise more caution in monetary matters. In this case the dream may be warning you to 'trim your sails', or not to 'sail too close to the wind'.

Undressing

Were you the one undressing in the dream? If so, what was the reason for removing your clothes? Was it to shock people? (see page 44). If you were undressing so that your clothes could be washed, it may suggest a desire to 'come clean' in some way other than physical. Or perhaps you are seeking to make changes, or improvements in your life (see also 'Nakedness', EMOTION & DESIRE, page 73).

Wading

If you were wading through water, was it clear or turbid? And what was the temperature of the water? If it was warm and pleasant, the dream could reflect friendship and contentment. Icy water may suggest an emotional life that is too cool. If you were wading through mud, it almost certainly represents anxiety (see page 47).

Walking

To dream of walking suggests steady – if not speedy – progress. If you were enjoying the walk, you are probably feeling relaxed and confident about your direction in life. Were you walking in the country? (see LANDSCAPE, page 80). Or were you making your way through a busy town? (see 'Traffic', ENVIRONMENT, page 75).

Washing

Washing yourself, or your own clothes, suggests a desire to make a fresh start. Or have you been flaunting some indiscretion – 'washing your dirty linen in public'? If you were using a washing machine that flooded, or broke down, it could indicate frustration (see also 'Machine', ACTIVITY OBJECTS, page 60).

Learn from your dreams what you lack.

W H Auden, 1945

Activity Objects

Brake

Braking a vehicle could be a suggestion to slow up in life – to 'put the brakes on'. Brakes that fail sometimes indicate insecurity, and may be a warning to consider any new offer carefully, as there could be hidden snags, (see 'Colin's Dream', page 56).

Harvest

What you were harvesting is important, as it is likely that you are now reaping what you have already sown. If it was a good harvest, your efforts have been productive and the benefits should be great. Increased security, knowledge and fulfilment are indicated. A poor harvest may suggest that more effort is required. Or perhaps what you have sown is not so desirable after all. (See also 'Grass', LANDSCAPE, page 81)

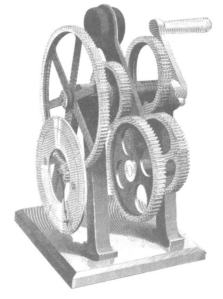

Machinery

This can be a symbol for the human body or mind, (Shakespeare's Hamlet referred to himself as a 'machine'). Was your own dream machinery running smoothly? Or was it rusty and inactive? If the latter, you may need to take mental or physical action in order to make progress.

Parachute

This could well be a 'flying' dream (see page 50), especially if you floated over houses or tree-tops before landing. If you jumped and the parachute opened immediately, it is an auspicious sign for plans and ambitions. If the parachute failed to open, it was a typical 'falling' dream (see page 51).

Saw

A saw is often considered to be a male sexual symbol, while the motion of sawing represents the sexual act. Who, if anyone, was with you in the dream? Of course, the dream need not be sexual, and may simply be reflecting a period of repetitive hard work.

Art & Entertainment

Actor/Actress

This dream could indicate that you need to 'be yourself' in waking life, and not try to play a part. Are you being quite sincere in a personal relationship, for instance? On the other hand, the dream could be encouraging you to be more assertive.

Film

Do not dismiss this dream if it obviously referred to a film you saw the previous evening. The unconscious is quite capable of using such recent - and seemingly insignificant – material to tell you something important about yourself. If you were watching a film and not involved in the action, you may be able to see things more objectively. The dream could be encouraging you to do just that.

Orchestra

Were you playing in the dream orchestra? If so, it could reflect your need to 'fit in' to society. If you were listening to an orchestra, how did the music relate to the mood of your life? Was it harmonious, or discordant?

Patterns

If the patterns consisted of curves, the dream may reflect your sexuality, or attitude to sex. If you were making a pattern, perhaps you were attempting to 'piece together' some aspect of your life. Were any particular colours predominant? (See COLOURS, page 67)

Television

If you were watching television in your dream, you may be trying to take a detached view of a problem. If you were watching yourself on the screen, you probably have the problem under control already. A blank or faulty screen suggests the need for more self-awareness (see also 'Film').

Theatre

The dream could suggest that you are 'making a drama' of something, perhaps unnecessarily. But if you are rather shy, it may be encouraging you to 'take centre stage' more often. Or were you stage managing the performance? If so, it could reflect the amount of control you have over other people.

Banquet
(see FOOD & DRINK, p79)
Magic
(see SUPERNATURAL & ETHEREAL, p90)
Party
(see ACTIVITY, p 58)
Photograph
(see POSSESSIONS, p87)

Authority

Executioner
(see THREAT, p92)
Learning
(see ACTIVITY, p58)
Punishment
(see THREAT, p93)
Royalty
(see PEOPLE, p84)
Undertaker
(see MORTALITY, p83)

Examination

If the examination was medical, it may reflect some hidden health fear. Otherwise, it suggests that you are being 'put to the test' in some way. But perhaps you are being over critical of yourself – or of someone else?

Government

To be 'in government', whether local or national, is a dream of power and may suggest that you are in control of your life. It could also be cautioning you against an attitude that is too autocratic. Perhaps you should look carefully at the opposition!

School

To dream of being back at school is quite common (see also 'Learning', ACTIVITY, page 58). Perhaps you feel a desire to solve the problems of adult life by fitting them into a structured framework. Do you think you lack confidence about your experience or knowledge? Or are you feeling reluctant to make a change? (See page 43).

Teacher

The dream teacher will almost certainly represent an authority figure. You may need to deal with a problem that goes back to your childhood – an inhibition, perhaps? But the dream could be telling you that there is something you have not yet 'grasped' (see also 'Learning', ACTIVITY, page 58).

Uniform

This dream may reflect your attitude to conformity. Were you pleased to see, or wear, the uniform and proud of what it represented? Or did you rebel against it? In either case, you need to decide whether your reaction was rational, or too extreme. The dream could have been suggesting childhood and the wearing of school uniform (see page 43).

Body

Back

If your back was painful in the dream, it could indicate some physical back trouble. But if you were feeling pleased with yourself it could be a pun dream, suggesting that you give yourself a 'pat on the back'. If you were carrying a back-breaking burden, it may suggest that you are taking on too many responsibilities.

Baldness

To dream of your own baldness could be a health warning. But it may be that you have recently suffered a lack of respect, or feel ashamed of something you have done. For men, dreaming of baldness may indicate fears of failing virility.

Blood

Blood is the symbol of life. If blood was flowing from you in the dream, perhaps you need to conserve your energy more carefully in waking life. If you were frightened of the blood, it may indicate that you are afraid to face up to something in your personal life. Blood can sometimes symbolize an inner truth. Perhaps you are not completely in control of your life, and need to be more positive?

Eyes

Eyes have been called the 'mirrors of the soul', so perhaps you are now looking more deeply within yourself. If you had something in your eye, it could be that you are encountering irritating obstacles. Or maybe you are not seeing things too clearly at the moment?

Face

This could be suggesting that you face up to your problems – or responsibilities. If you were looking at your own face in the mirror, your reflection may have hinted at your opinion of yourself.

Hair

This dream may be an indication of self-esteem. Thick, beautiful hair is a boost to the ego, while falling hair can symbolize a loss of self-respect. If you were combing or brushing your hair, it could suggest that you are seeking a solution to an annoying problem.

I dreamt that my hair was kemp, Then I dreamt that my true love unkempt it.
Ogden Nash, 1961.

Jaws

Were the jaws presented in the form of a nightmare – those of a monster, for example? If so, it could be a warning not to spread, or encourage malicious gossip. To dream of your own jaw may suggest a reluctance to 'speak out' about something. Or perhaps you have been talking too much!

Legs

If you were striding out, or 'standing on your own legs', the dream suggests progress and confidence. But if your legs were weak, or gave way under you, the reverse may be true. Perhaps you feel you 'haven't a leg to stand on' over some issue?

Skeleton

Have you had to get down to the 'bare bones' of a problem lately? Or was your dream skeleton in a cupboard? If the latter, it may allude to some guilty secret you are hiding. The dream could be cautioning you against overspending by hinting that 'lean times' are ahead!

Teeth

A tooth, or teeth, falling out in your dream could suggest a loss of self-respect (see page 47). To dream of false teeth may suggest that you need helping out of a difficult situation. Broken teeth are sometimes associated with the deterioration of existing relationships.

Urine

To dream of urinating, or searching for an appropriate place in which to urinate, is not uncommon. The most obvious explanation is a need to empty the bladder. However, some ancient oracles saw urine as a symbol of increasing creative power. To urinate in a dream could also signify a release from tension or worry.

Business & Finance

Debt

This dream may indicate the need to 'pay up' and face the music, or it may signal a desire to 'get even' with someone. Something in your life could be in need of correction. Perhaps you are demanding too much of other people. Or are they demanding too much of you?

Figures

If you work with figures, this could be an occupational 'Shared Anxiety Dream' (see page 48). It may suggest that you find it difficult to 'unwind'. But it could represent an obsessional problem, or hint that you are being rather too materialistic.

Money

There could be a connection with money problems in waking life. However, the dream was more likely to be telling you something about your emotional or sexual life. Were you being mean, or generous, with the money? Were you spending too much – or were you, perhaps, trying to save too carefully?

Office

If it was the office in which you work, and you were in any way worried by what you were doing, this could be another occupational anxiety dream (see page 48). However, it is more likely to refer to some aspect of your personality, or to the way you conduct your daily affairs.

Stock Market

This dream may reflect a financial venture that you are contemplating. Or it could be warning you against taking unnecessary risks. Are you worried about managing your financial affairs? Or is something other than money at risk in your life?

Wage

Wages in life represent a return for output or enterprise. Are you feeling 'short changed' in some way? The dream could indicate that you are putting much more into a relationship than you are getting from it. Perhaps it is 'pay off' time, and the relationship should end!

Operation
(see THREAT, page 93)

*For I did dream
of money-bags
tonight.*
William Shakespeare,
The Merchant of Venice

Captivity & Restriction

Cage

Are you feeling restricted or inhibited in life? To dream that you are imprisoned in a cage may indicate that a part of your personality is crying out for release. If you feel secure within your cage, you may be seeking personal reassurance, or comfort. Or are you imprisoning someone else? The characters sharing your dream are always significant.

Cave
(see LANDSCAPE, p 80)
Maze
(see LANDSCAPE, p81)
Punishment
(see THREAT, p93)
Tunnel
(see ENVIRONMENT, p75)
Web
(see EMOTION & DESIRE, p73)
Zoo
(see ENVIRONMENT, p75)
Vault
(see MORTALITY, p83)

Dungeon

This could be an obstacle dream, suggesting that you need to exert more effort in some endeavour. If you were unable to get out of the dungeon, it may be beneficial to consider a change of plan. If you escaped, however, you should achieve your aims by diligent effort.

Gag

Possibly an obstacle dream, but if you got rid of the gag or managed to speak through it, you will probably overcome your difficulties. However, the dream may be suggesting that you should keep quiet about something. Or perhaps you are feeling restrained about making a declaration that is important to you?

Key

The key is considered to be a sexual symbol. Both 'unlocking' and 'opening' are images with strong sexual connotations, especially for women. For a man to dream of losing a key could suggest anxiety about sexual prowess. But the key may also represent the solution to a waking problem, in which case losing it could imply frustration.

Lock

Freud sees the lock as a female sexual symbol. The dream may well indicate some sexual inhibition and the need to 'unlock' it. There could also be problems you are 'locked into', or aspects of life from which you feel 'locked out'.

Prison

To dream of being imprisoned may be a sign of oppression. Are you feeling 'trapped' or 'shut-in'? Perhaps your life seems rather claustrophobic at present? There could also be some element of your personality that you seem unable to 'release'.

Colours

Black

If there was something predominantly black in your dream it could symbolize a 'void', and possibly suggest a lack of knowledge, or confidence. Black also represents the underworld in many cultures, and may signify some aspect of secrecy in waking life. Seen or worn at a funeral, however, it has quite a different connotation, and can indicate change of circumstances or good news.

Blue

This colour signifies truth, justice and inner spirituality. If it featured prominently in your dream it may suggest a need to relax and be a little more meditative. Or have you been 'feeling blue' lately?

Green

Generally speaking, our awareness of colour in waking life influences the effect of colour in our dreams. Green, the colour of vegetation, hope and abundance, is very much part of life and represents nature in its simplest forms. However, it could signify being 'green' in judgement, and may indicate the need for more maturity.

Red

To dream in well defined colour is thought to be a sign of vitality, and red is regarded by Hindus as representing the energy force of life. It is a very positive colour, associated with festivity, love and sexual passion – but also with cruelty. It can, of course, be a warning, signalling us to 'stop'!

Yellow

Bright yellow represents intuition, faith and goodness, symbolized by the light of the sun. It is also associated with health and well-being, so this could be a most auspicious dream. But to dream of dark, muddy yellow can suggest secrecy, betrayal or avarice.

White

A colour associated with simplicity and spiritual authority, it is as positive as black is negative. However, it is also equated with chastity and purification of the soul, so a white dominated dream could suggest that you are distancing yourself from problems and reality!

Communication

Angel
(see SUPERNATURAL &
ETHEREAL, p90)
Book
(see POSSESSIONS, p85)
Learning
(see ACTIVITY, p58)
Library
(see ENVIRONMENT, p74)
Map
(see POSSESSIONS, p86)
Pen/Pencil
(see POSSESSIONS, p86)
Visit
(see RELATIONSHIP, p89)

Appointment

Were you keeping an appointment or breaking one? The dream could be warning you to reconsider a plan, or telling you to face up to your waking problems. The person with whom you made the appointment could be significant.

Label

Are you, perhaps, afraid of being considered a stereotype? The dream could suggest that you feel yourself 'labelled' for a particular trait, or characteristic. Maybe you need to assert yourself more, and express your individuality. An incorrectly addressed, or loose label may indicate that you have lost direction in some way.

Letter

This is an obvious 'message' dream. However, our dreams are always trying to tell us something, so the contents of the letter are important (see also 'Angel', SUPERNATURAL & ETHEREAL, page 90). If the letter came from a distance – overseas, perhaps – it could be reminding you nostalgically of an old friend or lover.

Newspaper

Were you reading the newspaper or wrapping something in it? Perhaps you were doing both? If so, think very carefully of any relationship there may have been between the newspaper headlines and the object that you were wrapping up.

Parcel

To dream of unpacking a parcel may indicate a period of self discovery. What was in the parcel? Your reaction to the contents could indicate your attitude to a current situation. If you were wrapping a parcel and the string failed to hold it together, you may be less in control than you thought.

Question

If you were being questioned in your dream, much depends upon whether or not you could give satisfactory answers. Perhaps you feel that your knowledge and experience are being challenged in some way? Or do you need to increase your understanding of other people? It could be your personal motivations that are 'in question'.

Telephone

This is an obvious message dream. Did you make the call, or receive it? The person to whom you were speaking could be relevant. Perhaps you have been thinking about them, or expecting to hear from them? If you had difficulty in making yourself heard, it may indicate a fear of failure (see page 48).

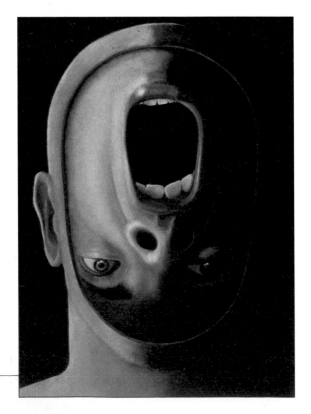

Domestic

Carpet

Walking along a carpet could represent your own progress. If the carpet was beautiful, it augurs success. If it was shabby or threadbare, perhaps you feel apprehensive about your next move. Or do you feel that you are facing trouble and may be 'on the carpet' for something?

Clock/Watch

This dream could be a straightforward warning to stop wasting time, by making you aware that 'time is slipping by'. Or it could, perhaps, be cautioning you against unpunctuality. On the other hand, maybe the 'time is ripe' to make a change in your life.

Cup

Full cups are said to indicate emotional fulfilment, and empty cups to represent emotional loss. An overflowing cup may be a warning that you are being swept away by your feelings and should try to be more objective.

Feathers

To dream of many feathers is considered a good omen. Feathers in a quilt represent warmth, comfort and security (but see also page 56). If the feathers were escaping, you may fear that your security is slipping. Exotic feathers such as peacock, or ostrich may suggest that you need more variety in your life.

Iron/Ironing

A metal iron is associated with strength, endurance and aggression. Perhaps you lack some of these qualities. Or do you possess them more forcibly than you should? If you dreamt that you were ironing, it could be a reference to 'ironing out' your problems.

Jug

The jug can be a sexual symbol, and in art it frequently represents virginity. If liquid was being poured from the jug in your dream, it may indicate that you are ready to 'give yourself' – or a part of yourself – to someone else.

Mattress

The interpretation of this dream depends very much on the condition of the mattress. If it was firm and supportive it could mean that you are receiving help and support from family, or a partner. If the mattress was uncomfortable, it may be reflecting your present domestic situation.

Mess

If you were able to clear up the mess efficiently, it may indicate an end to a worrying or 'messy' situation in waking life. If you made the mess and other people were offended, it could suggest feelings of social inadequacy (see page 46).

Quilt

A quilt usually signifies comfort, warmth and protection. Do you feel a lack of any of these things? If you were really snug and comfortable under your dream quilt, the chances are that you feel secure in a domestic situation. If the quilt had a complex pattern, it may suggest that you are creating complications in life.

Kitchen

The kitchen, being the source of heat and food, represents a central part of the dreamer's being (see page 38). If you were happily employed in your kitchen, you have little to worry about. Problems with the cooker or fire, however, may relate to your health in some way.

Ladder

A symbol Freud associated with sexual intercourse. If you climb the ladder successfully, the implication is obvious. If you fall off, or encounter broken rungs, it may indicate worries about sexual adequacy. Climbing a ladder can also symbolize ambition and the quest for happiness.

Lamp

This is usually a positive dream. Lamplight can symbolize spiritual or intellectual illumination. It also offers guidance and reassurance. If your dream lamp goes out, this could suggest disappointment in waking life. Or perhaps you are not seeing things too clearly at the moment (see also 'Light', ELEMENTS, page 71).

Table

If the table bore food, or was having food prepared on it, see 'Banquet' and 'Kitchen'. If a meeting was taking place round the table, the people present could represent aspects of your own character. But the dream could have been hinting that you should be more open, and 'put your cards on the table'.

Vacuum/Vacuum Cleaner

To dream of using a vacuum cleaner could suggest you are 'spring cleaning' – mentally or physically. You may be getting rid of old ideas and attitudes, and sorting out your problems. If you dreamt you were 'in a vacuum', it could suggest that you feel isolated and alone.

Elements

Electricity

Do you need to expend more energy in waking life? Perhaps you are lacking 'power' in some way? The dream could be hinting that you need to 'recharge your batteries'. A power cut, or failing electricity supply usually indicates frustration in wishes or desires, (see also 'Robert's Dream', page 41).

Fire

To dream of lighting a fire may suggest the need to start on some project in waking life. If you are 'playing with fire' in any way it is possibly a pun dream, but could signify that you are taking unnecessary risks. A 'raging inferno' may be cautioning you to exercise more control. Fire also has strong creative elements and could be hinting the need for more self expression.

Ice

Are you, perhaps, walking on ice? Or does the temperature of ice refer to the state of your emotions? The dream could indicate that you are not expressing yourself in a fulfilling manner. Or maybe you are going through an unsettling experience, and feel as if you are on 'a slippery slope'.

Light

This dream nearly always refers to spiritual or psychological illumination. The colour of the light could be important. A warm, glowing light is usually positive, and indicates security and confidence. A red light can be a warning. For some people, however, it may also have sexual connotations. (See also 'Lamp', DOMESTIC, page 70).

Night

If the night was very dark, it could reflect your present mood. If you were lost in the dream, it may indicate that you need to re-examine your direction in life. An ending to a long night could signify the end of a problem. And a moonlit night may suggest romance (See also 'Darkness', THREAT, page 91).

Thunder

Traditionally symbolizing the anger of the gods, this dream could represent your inner anger. Perhaps some action of your own has evoked that anger? If you were afraid of the thunder, you may be in some fear of your emotions. But make sure that a real thunder storm during the night did not intrude into your dreams!

Water

An unchecked flood or waterfall suggests the need for more restraint. To dream of water being confined could hint that more emotional freedom is required. Your own attitude to water is important. However, to most of us a calm lake in a beautiful setting represents tranquillity.

Someone dreamt that the sky was destroyed. He died.
Artemidorus, AD150

Emotion & Desire

Bedfellow
(see RELATIONSHIPS, p83)
Embrace (
see RELATIONSHIPS, p88)
Invisibility
(see SUPERNATURAL &
ETHEREAL, p90)
Learning
(see ACTIVITY, p58)
Pain
(see THREAT, page 93)
Youth
(see PEOPLE, p84)

*That some have
never dreamed is
as improbable as
that some have
never laughed.*
Sir Thomas Browne, 1650

Change

Dreams have the magical quality of transformation – anything can change into something else. A heavy burden may change into a more desirable load, indicating a changing attitude towards waking responsibilities. But if a colourful object changes into something dull, it could suggest a lack of assertiveness or concentration.

Disappointment

Some dream interpreters regard this as a dream of opposite meaning and claim that it indicates success. However, if the dream left you feeling depressed, take steps to examine any circumstances in waking life that could lead to disappointment. Could some inner weakness be getting the better of you, perhaps?

Floating

If you were floating without difficulty it is a very good omen. It implies that you are on top of your problems and enjoying what life has to offer. Floating may offer similar sensations to flying (see page 51) but the dreamer's connection with water could suggest rather less freedom.

Grief

If you experienced feelings of overwhelming grief in your dream, something in waking life may be distressing you more than you realize. Perhaps you should try to express your grief more openly. The dream may also reflect lost innocence, or ideals.

Jealousy

Feelings of jealousy in a dream can usually be related to similar feelings in waking life. Who were you jealous of, and what did they do to cause your jealousy? It is important to try to make the dream 'connection', and discover the true source of this negative emotion.

Laughter

Some interpreters regard this as a dream of opposite meaning, unless the laughter is that of children. Children's laughter indicates happiness and good fortune. Adult laughter may suggest disappointment or sorrow. Our own dream laughter invariably wakes us up (see 'Alison's Dream', page 45) but the joke rarely survives the light of day.

Waiting

What were you waiting for in your dream? Did you feel excited, or were you bored and resentful? Perhaps there is something that relates to these feelings in your waking life? If you were 'waiting' on table, it may indicate a desire to help someone.

Web

A web may signify the meshes of an intrigue. Or perhaps you need to try new ventures and fresh challenges – to 'clear the cobwebs' from your life. If there was a spider in the web, what was your reaction to it? If you were really frightened, this could have been a small 'monster' dream.

Weeping

This can sometimes manifest itself as a 'mood' dream, creating a feeling of sadness that remains with us on waking. Your tears may have had a healing quality, washing away negative emotions that had been troubling you in life. If someone else was weeping in the dream, it could indicate that a friend is in need of your support.

Nakedness

It is nearly always the dreamer who is naked, so your reaction to the situation is important. If you were embarrassed, it may suggest inhibitions in waking life. If you were enjoying your nakedness, perhaps you feel restricted in some way and need to 'break out'! (See also page 44).

Search

Occasionally, a dream may enable us to locate an object we have really lost, or mislaid. More often, however, the dream 'search' will reflect an emotional loss. Perhaps there is something you feel the need to replace in your life?

Thirst

What you were thirsting for in the dream is important. If it was water, it may suggest that your life is a little dull at present, and needs enlivening or 'refreshing'. If you quenched your thirst at a well or a spring, it could indicate spiritual or emotional fulfilment.

Environment

Abbey

Looking up at an abbey or cathedral in a dream may relate to ambitious aspirations. If you felt inspired or elated it bodes well for your ambitions. But if you were frightened, it could mean that you are aiming too high.

Building

The building represents the dreamer, and the dreamer's achievements. Awe inspiring buildings such as castles and mansions are usually related to ambition, but marble halls may be a warning of pomposity. Discovering empty rooms in a house suggests a readiness for new intellectual challenges. Climbing stairs, according to Freud, is always a sexual image.

Castle

Are you building 'castles in the air' and aiming too high? Perhaps you are unduly houseproud, or want to be more dominant in your own home. Remember the childhood chant, 'I'm the King of the Castle'? A castle in ruins could hint that perhaps you should curb any destructive passions.

Hall

A hall, town hall or similar structure, suggests that you are well-tuned to your community. An empty hall may represent an unexplored area of your personality. If there were other people in the hall, your attitude to their presence could be important.

Library

Were you searching for a particular book and unable to find it? If so, the dream could indicate frustration, or possibly an under-developed aspect of your own character. The library itself symbolizes stored knowledge, so you may need to draw on the experience you have acquired over the years.

Park/Parking

If you were feeling relaxed and at ease in your dream park, it is a good omen. But if you were trespassing, perhaps you are encroaching on someone else's territory in life? To have parked your car illegally, or to have forgotten where you parked it, could suggest a rash action or illicit affair.

Quay

Were there ships alongside your dream quay? Ships can symbolize the state of our emotions, so their size and condition may be relevant. If the quay was empty, it could suggest that you are going through a period of idleness, or that you are neglecting something important in your life.

Tower

A tower can be a phallic symbol. If you were climbing steps inside the tower, the dream almost certainly has sexual connotations (see 'Simon's Dream', page 53). Towers are also features of many religious buildings, and to be looking up at one may indicate ambition.

Traffic

To watch traffic in a dream may indicate that you are trying to solve a problem alone, when you should be requesting help. If you were driving a car that was involved in a traffic jam, it could suggest frustration in waking life.

Tunnel

This is quite a common dream, and Freud regarded it as a vaginal symbol (see page 44). Were you entering, or leaving the tunnel? Could you see the light at the end of it? If so, it is a good sign, as the tunnel may represent a period of anxiety through which you are passing.

Zoo

How you felt about the animals at the zoo is important. Did you envy their protected state? Or did you feel they represented your own need to be released? (see also 'Cage', CAPTIVITY & RESTRICTION, page 66). Were you a keeper at the zoo? If so, this could reflect a desire to be more in control of your life.

Fish, Flesh & Fowl
(Animal Kingdom)

Feathers
(see DOMESTIC, p69)
Zoo
(see ENVIRONMENT, p75)

Birds

Birds are usually considered a fortunate dream omen. Like angels, they can represent messengers. They can also symbolize the freedom associated with flying. However, if the birds in your dream were caged, it may suggest that you lack a freedom of spirit which you crave. Smaller, garden birds may be related to home and family life, especially if you were feeding them.

Cat

Cats often symbolize elegant feminity. They are highly sensual and may represent something that you desire. But the cat can quickly turn from a warm, purring creature to an aggressive hunter. If the cat snarls and shows its claws, the dream may suggest that you should be more assertive in waking life.

Dog

A symbol of loyalty and devotion, which could also suggest an excess of these emotions. Friendship is strongly indicated if you love dogs, and the possibility of a warning if you fear them. A pun is always possible, of course. Have you been 'barking up the wrong tree' recently?

Eagle

A strong dream symbol, usually indicating power and independence. A soaring eagle may foretell success and prosperity. But the eagle is also a bird of prey, so perhaps your behaviour to others is a little threatening. Or are you feeling threatened yourself? A sitting or perching eagle could suggest that you are biding your time before making a decision.

Elephant

This magnificent creature usually represents health and friendship. Even an attacking elephant indicates no more than a temporary obstacle to your progress. But 'an elephant never forgets', so could you be harbouring a grievance?

Fish/Fishing

To see fish swimming in clear water is a good omen, suggesting that you are acquiring deeper self-knowledge. If you were fishing, what you caught (if anything) is important. Carp represent a warning against too much self-criticism. Dead fish may indicate disappointment in your life.

Horse

The horse is a symbol of beauty and power, and represents progress and controlled strength. If you were riding the horse, there may be sexual overtones. Or perhaps you were 'riding out' a problem? The dream may well refer to your inner power, energy and progress.

Insects

This could be an obstacle dream. If you succeeded in getting rid of the insects, it could mean that you will overcome your difficulties more easily than you thought. Recurring dreams of insects may suggest that you feel

something in your life is under attack. Scorpions can represent verbal attacks.

Kangaroo

A kangaroo with young in pouch is usually a symbol of maternity. Are you being overprotective towards your children? Or, conversely, are you seeking too much protection for yourself? Then again, the dream may suggest that you are making progress in 'leaps and bounds'.

Lion

The lion is a very positive image, symbolizing strength, mastery, pride and desire. But remember that it can be dangerous, and that it devours its prey. Are you being unduly masterful at present? The lion is also regal and dignified. Do you envy these qualities, or are you, perhaps, exhibiting them yourself to an undesirable degree?

Pig

This could suggest selfish or chauvinistic behaviour on someone's part. It could also be a pun dream. Are you facing the consequences of an indiscretion, and feel you must 'save your bacon'? Or have you spent money unwisely, and fear that you have bought a 'pig in a poke'?

'Do you ever have any good sex dreams?'
My fish dream is a sex dream
Joseph Heller,
Catch 22, 1961

Rats

To dream of rats may indicate enemies in life. Or have you been disloyal to someone? If you were aggressive towards the rat, it suggests that you are able to cope with the problem.

Snake

An ancient symbol with many meanings. It can suggest the power of sexuality – Freud's snakes, of course, were always sexual symbols (see page 44). The dream snake may also represent spiritual energy, and can convey wisdom and healing. If you were frightened of the snake, however, it may indicate anxiety or frustration about your sex life.

A man dreamt that he slipped out of his flesh just as a snake sheds its old skin.

Artemidorus, AD150

Pigeons

Usually an auspicious dream. Pigeons make good parents, and to dream of them may suggest warmth and reassurance in the home, or from the family. Loyalty in love is often symbolized by these birds. Pigeons can also be carriers, so perhaps some special news is indicated.

Swan

These beautiful creatures often symbolize happiness. Were you the swan in your dream? You are probably seeing yourself as elegant and calm but capable of aggression – a satisfying personal view, so long as you avoid smugness. If the swan was black, you may be seeing yourself at variance with other people.

Wolf

If the wolf was threatening you, this could be a very frightening dream. As with all worrying dreams, it represents an anxiety in waking life, and identifying it is most important. There may, of course, be financial implications – perhaps you are trying to 'keep the wolf from the door'?

Zebra

To dream of any animal usually represents our basic 'animal instincts'. But the unusual, striped appearance of the zebra may relate to something different (see also 'Patterns', ART & ENTERTAINMENT, page 61). Perhaps the dream suggests a zebra crossing, and a desire for a temporary halt to the hustle of life.

Food & Drink

Alcohol

This dream strongly suggests physical pleasure. If you were taking alcohol in moderation it could imply confidence and success. To take it in excess, however, may be a warning to keep to the simple pleasures in life, and to avoid getting involved in embarrassing situations.

Banquet

If you are on a diet this may well be a wish-fulfilment dream. However, it could be a warning against overindulgence and lack of self-restraint in waking life. If you were nibbling fastidiously, it suggests you may be holding back in an emotional involvement. If no one offered you food at the banquet, it could indicate frustration with plans or relationships.

Cake

Are you trying to 'have your cake and eat it'? Or perhaps you want to enjoy the 'icing on the cake' of success. A 'slice of cake' could refer to an aspect of your personality and how you express yourself to other people.

Eggs

Freud considered the egg to be a sexual symbol. It is certainly associated with new beginnings, birth and fertility. The delicacy of the egg could also represent the frailty of a relationship. Or perhaps you are being warned not to 'put all your eggs in one basket'.

Milk

A dream with maternal implications. Did someone require the 'milk of human kindness' from you, and were you supplying it to them in the dream? If you were drinking milk it could suggest that you feel in need of sustenance of some kind – not necessarily physical.

Nuts

To dream of cracking nuts invariably means that there is a waking problem to be 'cracked'. If there were many nuts, or they were difficult to crack, it may represent the extent of the problem.

Wine

This dream usually symbolizes health and generosity. To drink rich, colourful wine suggests the acquisition of emotional experience. Bottles of wine often represent those wiser than ourselves, and spilt wine may indicate a disappointment.

Apple
(see LANDSCAPE, p80)
Eating
(see ACTIVITY, p57)

Landscape

Apple/Apple Tree

Tasting a delicious apple suggests an acute sexual appetite – a desire to 'savour the fruits of life', perhaps. There may well be an association with anyone sharing the dream with you. To dream of an apple tree in blossom promises joy. William Golding described apple-blossom as 'a cloud of angels flashing in the sunlight.' To dream of a crab-apple tree indicates a new experience.

Cave

A symbol of female sexuality, indicating the security of the womb. The dream suggests a need to shelter from someone, or something. Perhaps you are not facing up to life's problems.

Cliff

This could be an obstacle dream and your reaction to the cliff is important. Were you attempting to climb it? Perhaps you are concerned with material progress and how to reach your objectives? If you felt exhilarated by your climb, this could be a good omen. But the dream may also be cautioning you against a 'fall'.

Countryside

To dream of a beautiful country scene is memorable and refreshing. But an unwelcome intruder in your scene could represent a disruptive influence in waking life. If the scene receded visually, it may indicate ambitions slipping out of reach, and if it was crowded, it could suggest that you are taking on too much.

Flowers

A dream associated with freshness and vitality, and one that suggests personal happiness. Flowers opening, or in bud may refer to your own developing awareness. The gathering of flowers is said to symbolize fulfilment.

Globe

The circle is a symbol of wholeness, and a globe could have the same encouraging implication. Perhaps you are taking a 'global' view of a problem? Or maybe you are riding high and feel that the world is yours? Of course, the dream could indicate a desire for travel and adventure.

Grass

If the grass was lush and green, it is a good omen and suggests the richness and fullness of your life at present. If you were cutting grass you could be 'reaping your own harvest' in some way. If you were sowing it, you are probably 'preparing the ground' for something important. If the ground was brown and parched, a much more determined effort is needed to get the most from life.

Island

This dream may suggest delightful solitude, or unpleasant isolation. How you felt about the island is important. The pleasure of being on a welcoming island may suggest that you need more time to yourself. But if the island was barren, could this reflect your life at the moment?

Jungle

This may be an obstacle dream, so try to relate it to a waking problem. Did you have to hack your way through the jungle? If the undergrowth was unduly thick, it could suggest you need to do some mental 'clearing' before taking the next steps.

Marsh

If you were sinking in the marsh, the dream could suggest that you are feeling very insecure. Are you being 'dragged down' by worries and anxieties? If you watched someone else sink in the marsh, this represents extreme anxiety on your part (see also 'Drowning', page 91).

Maze

Are you finding waking life confusing? The maze could reflect your bewilderment. Perhaps the dream is a hint that you should slow up and 'take your bearings'. If you found your way out of the maze it is a positive sign, and suggests that you are in control.

Orchard

Was your dream orchard shady, with many trees? This could indicate that you are seeking mental shelter. Perhaps you feel the need to be protected from a waking problem? If the orchard was fruitful, you may be looking for sustenance – but, of course, it need not be physical.

Quarry

If the quarry was a hole in the landscape, from which soil, gravel or slate had been removed, the dream may symbolize something that has left a 'gap' in you life. If you were doing the quarrying, it could indicate the extent to which you are using your mental resources.

The quaint mazes in the wanton green For lack of tread are indistinguishable.
William Shakespeare,
A Midsummer Night's Dream

Sea

The sea is a powerful symbol, and represents part of our 'collective unconscious'. Deep emotions and maternal instincts, or a relationship with the dreamer's mother, are probably involved. Was the sea rough or calm in your dream, and what was your reaction to it? (see also 'Water', ELEMENTS, page 71).

Tree

A strong dream symbol, representing wisdom and knowledge. Trees offer protection, shade and sustenance and the dream could refer to family members or close friends. Blossoming trees usually represent happiness (see 'Apple Tree'). If you felt intimidated by the trees, it may be a comment on your sexuality, or spiritual growth.

Vine/Vineyard

Vines may be fruitful, but they are also clinging. Your dream could indicate an element of claustrophobia. On the other hand, the grapevine is associated with sexual experience and a free expression of emotion. Perhaps the dream is suggesting that you need more freedom, despite the richness of the vine.

Volcano

The dream could be inviting you to 'let off steam'! Perhaps you feel that you have been 'sitting on a volcano', and things are about to erupt? But if you are going to 'blow your top', remember that others could suffer in the lava of your fury.

Rocks

A single large rock, or boulder may represent security. If it was blocking your path, however, it suggests an obstruction to your objectives. Smaller rocks indicate minor difficulties. If you were throwing the rocks, perhaps you need to release anger.

Sand

Loose sand that shifted beneath your feet suggests uncertainty in waking life. If you were looking across the sand from a vantage point – a beach, or clifftop – the dream may represent a situation that you need to assess. If you stepped into quicksands, it could indicate stress or anxiety (see also 'Marsh').

Mortality

Corpse

Usually a dream of opposite meaning, and often a transformation dream, indicating that some change is about to take place in the dreamer's life. The 'body', even if it someone you know, will always represent an aspect of yourself.

Death

This is not a negative symbol but, again, implies change and transformation. Your unconscious may have noted some deep psychological change – in yourself or in someone else – that your conscious mind was unaware of. Death is also considered a dream of opposite meaning, and could foretell the news of a birth.

Funeral

Another dream of opposite meaning, and usually a very positive omen. It represents change and new beginnings and sometimes heralds tidings of a birth. You are now ready for new commitments and experiences, and may be changing your attitudes and your outlook on life in general.

Grave

The circumstances of the dream may link it with 'Death' or 'Funeral', both of which are positive omens and indicate new beginnings. However, it could be a warning to take a waking situation more 'gravely', or seriously.

Undertaker

The implication is change, not gloom. The undertaker in your dream may have represented a figure of authority – someone, perhaps, who can help you through a period of transformation, or self discovery. The dream could also suggest the passing of time.

Vault

Families are laid to rest in vaults. so could you be laying a family problem 'to rest'? Perhaps you are interested in genealogy and are researching into your family history – or would like to do so?

Execution/Executioner
(see THREAT, p92)
Gallows
(see THREAT, p92)
Hearse
(see TRANSPORT, p94)
Killing
(see THREAT, p92)

Now is the time of night
That the graves, all gaping wide,
Every one lets forth his sprite.
William Shakespeare,
A Midsummer Night's Dream

People

Baby

To dream of a baby usually means that you are acknowledging new responsibilities in your life. The baby may also symbolize a developing idea or concept. If you want children, this could be a straightforward wish-fulfilment dream.

Child/Children

One child may represent you, in which case your attitude could indicate your own self-confidence – or lack of it. Did you love and nurture the child, or did you scorn it? It could, of course, represent an immature side to your own personality. To dream of several children can be a sign of happiness.

Girl

To dream of a young girl whom you recognize is considered a good omen, with encouraging prospects. Any female figure appearing in a dream can represent the feminine side of your own personality. But for a man to dream of being a girl could suggest a latent sexual problem.

Martyr

Are you being a martyr in some way? If so, is your martyrdom really helping anyone? Almost certainly it will not be helping you! Perhaps you are defending a particular principle, or point-of-view, to the bitter end. The dream may be hinting that you should be a little easier on yourself.

Royalty

A dream of royalty is quite common, and often takes the form of a personal meeting. According to Freud, the king or queen represent the dreamer's parents, while a

prince or princess represents the dreamer. But it is likely that you will identify with some aspect of any royal personality in your dream. If you are shy, this could be encouraging you to have more self-esteem.

Youth

According to Jung, the youth represents potential and innocence – the chance for a new start. But it could be wish-fulfilment if you dreamed of your own youth, or of being much younger than you are.

Possessions

Bag

To dream of a full bag is considered auspicious. If you were putting things in a bag, you may be putting things aside in waking life. If you were packing a travelling bag it could indicate a journey – or simply the wish to get away.

Book

A dream concerned with memories, knowledge and past experiences. Progress may be indicated, or perhaps you are learning more about yourself at this time. The dream could suggest that you take your present situation more seriously.

Clothes

Wearing outlandish or unsuitable garments may indicate that you are 'putting on an act' in waking life. Buying original clothing could be a hint to change your image. The colour, or colours of the clothes in your dream could be relevant (see COLOURS, page 67). But if your outfit felt comfortable and 'right', you are probably ready to face the world.

Diamonds

This may be a straightforward wish-fulfilment dream. But the purity of the diamond could reflect on the conception you have of your own perfection – or imperfections. The dream may indicate a desire for material security, or a need for you to deepen emotional relationships (see also 'Jewels').

Doll

Dream dolls, being symbols of childhood, frequently refer to some aspect of immaturity in the dreamer. It could be a warning to take your role in life more seriously. Or perhaps you lack assertiveness, and are allowing yourself to be manipulated like a doll, or a puppet.

Rolls-Royce
(see TRANSPORT, p94)

Gloves

Gloves may represent security, but they are also regarded as sexual symbols. A glove with a hole in it, a lost glove, or a carefully dropped glove each has a 'sex signal' association for women. For men, the dream could mean that they should be examining their attitude toward the opposite sex.

Hat

What sort of hat was it in your dream? Was the colour significant? (see 'Jean's Dream', page 43). A hat can alter the appearance and often seems to change the personality. Perhaps your dream was telling you that you have a desire to do just that!

Jewels

To wear, or possess beautiful jewels may be a wish-fulfilment dream. There could also be a hint of vanity involved. If the jewels were unattainable, it may suggest that you are setting yourself standards you cannot achieve. But perhaps the 'jewels' represent some spiritual quality you have overlooked (see also 'Diamonds').

Map

This could be a symbol of orientation, implying that you are confident about your position in a current situation. But if you are feeling you have 'lost your way', the dream map may equally well symbolize disorientation! Try to recall what the map meant to you, and how thoroughly you were studying it.

Mirror

This may be a dream of opposite meaning. The mirror image is always reversed, and your dream could have been reversing reality. So even if the reflection was very unpleasant, things may not be nearly so bad as they seem! A broken mirror could suggest that you feel 'shattered' about something (see also 'Face', BODY, page 63).

Ornament

What happened to the ornament in your dream? Was it admired, or put away, unwanted? The ornament could represent you. Are you seeking admiration, or afraid of being 'put in the shade' by someone? If the ornament was broken, it may suggest a need to re-examine your attitudes.

Pen/Pencil

These may be obvious phallic symbols, but the dream need not necessarily be sexual. However, if you were sharpening a pencil or filling a pen, it does suggest sexual connotations. Perhaps what you were writing has some special significance for you?

Photograph

Were you taking the photograph? If so, perhaps there is a situation in life that you need to get 'in focus'. Or are you keen to remember something, or someone? To dream of tearing up an old photograph usually indicates a desire to escape from the past, and to live in the present.

Umbrella

If the umbrella in your dream was open in a shower, or rainstorm, it represents protection. You may be seeking the protection yourself, or offering it to someone else. If the umbrella was blown inside out, it could indicate a change in your life. If you lost the umbrella, perhaps you fear being abandoned by someone?

Veil

The veil represents the feminine side of the dreamer's personality. It can indicate that you are concealing aspects of your character – perhaps even from yourself. Veils may be intriguing, but they are also associated with the rejection of worldly objectives. It may be important to decide who, or what was behind the veil.

Relationships

Adultery

To dream of committing adultery suggests that there is a problem in your relationship. Or it may hint that you should be rather careful when choosing a confidante. Fidelity dreams do not always indicate relationships with other people, however, and may mean that your own strength of purpose is being tested.

Bedfellow

This may be a sexual dream, in which case the interpretation is straightforward. However, the 'bedfellow' may represent some inner conflict, or the dream could be telling you something about an existing partnership.

Enemy
(see THREAT, p92)

*I dreamt we were
both in a bed of
roses, almost
smothered.*

Robert Herrick, 1648

Embrace

A pleasurable embrace may reflect the degree of your inner contentment. Or it could be encouraging you to love yourself more. If you were doing the embracing, it may suggest that you are in need of love and affection. An unpleasant or frightening embrace could be warning you to examine carefully any undesirable element, or scheme that is 'embracing' you in waking life.

Family

What does the family represent to you, personally – warmth and security, or rivalry and antagonism? The dream will reflect these emotions in your own life. Individual family members may be presented as an extension of your own personality. If you recognize this, you can achieve a greater understanding of yourself and your family.

Falsehood

Are you, perhaps, deceiving yourself about something? It may be a wrongly made decision that you are trying to 'cover up', or an aspect of your own personality that you prefer to see in a more favourable light. You may be deceiving someone else, of course.

Lie

Were you telling the lie? Or was someone lying to you? The type of lie is important. Was it vicious? Or simply told in order to 'save face' – either your own, or someone else's? It could be a pun dream, telling you to 'lie low', or to 'let sleeping dogs lie'.

Marriage

Marriage symbolizes a 'joining together' and this may indicate a 'marriage' between two areas of your own personality. It could, of course, be a wish-fulfilment dream. Or perhaps you are about to go into partnership, sign a contract or make some other form of commitment?

Nagging

Were you doing the nagging? If so, you were probably using the dream as a safety valve to 'let off steam' over some resentment. If you were being nagged, it could be a hint to change your lifestyle, or your attitude to something.

Neighbours

How you feel about your neighbourhood may have some bearing on this dream. It is likely that the 'neighbours' represent an aspect of your own life. If the relationship was friendly, it suggests that you are coping well with a situation that is particularly close to you. But

if you were quarrelling with your dream neighbours, you may need to view things more rationally.

Quarrel

How you felt on waking is very important with this type of dream. If you experienced a sense of release, the quarrel could have 'cleared the air' and allowed you to get rid of negative emotions. But your dream may have represented an inner conflict, which you still need to resolve.

Visit

Have you been neglecting friends or relations? The dream could be reminding you of duty visits, or cautioning you against losing contact with those you hold dear. If you dreamt of visiting strange countries, it could suggest that you need fresh challenges in your life.

Wedding

Those taking part in the wedding could be important to the interpretation of the dream. Could the clergyman have represented your father, or some other authority figure in your life? Who else was present? If the wedding was disrupted in any way, there may be conflicts to resolve before you can feel 'at one' with yourself.

What, was I married to her in my dream?
William Shakespeare,
Comedy of Errors

Darkness
(see THREAT, p91)
Night
(see ELEMENTS, p71)
Wheel
(see TRANSPORT, p94)

Supernatural & Ethereal

Angel

This is usually a favourable dream. Were you the angel? If so, it could indicate that you will rise to a higher status. On the other hand, perhaps you should beware of getting 'above yourself'. If you saw angels, they could represent messengers and the interpretation must be based on their demeanour.

Ghost

Were you the ghost in the dream? If so, it may suggest that you are disregarding your health in some way – that you are, in fact, a 'mere ghost' of your former self. If it was the ghost of someone else, it could be a 'cry for help' from the person indicated.

Invisibility

This is not a common dream, and may be wish-fulfilment. Do you long for obscurity in waking life? Do you, perhaps, dislike being noticed because you are unduly shy? The dream may indicate that you need to acquire more confidence and to start appreciating your true worth.

Magic

The dream could be reflecting your own feelings at this time. Are you elated – in love perhaps – and finding everything 'magic'? Or are you mystified about something? Magic can be tricky, and even dangerous. Have you been 'up to tricks' recently, or is someone else being 'tricky', and deceiving you?

Shadow

According to Jung, a dream shadow represents the inferior parts of our personality – those things we refuse to acknowledge about ourselves. Such traits are usually incompatible with our true nature, so if we study the dream carefully it could help us to find means of self improvement.

Threat

This accident is not unlike my dream.
William Shakespeare, *Othello*

Abandon

If you were behaving in an 'abandoned', or loose, manner it could mean you need to express yourself more freely. To be abandoned by someone else may be a hint to rid yourself of a problem. But if you were abandoned by someone you find disagreeable in waking life, you are possibly dealing with the problem already.

Accident

Exercise extra caution if the dream situation occurs in waking life, as it may be a warning. However, it could refer to a personal mistake. Note carefully the people involved in the dream accident and decide if they are likely to obstruct your progress in any situation in which you are involved.

Amputation

This is sometimes considered to be a dream of opposite meaning – the loss of a limb indicating a forthcoming gain, or promotion. But it could also mean that a relationship is about to end, or to take a turn for the worse.

Danger

This could be a warning dream, so carefully consider it in connection with all aspects of your waking life. If you face the dream danger, it is usually a sign that you will overcome your difficulties.

Darkness

This is often a rather unpleasant 'mood' dream, and could reflect your present state of mind. Are you feeling depressed, or pessimistic? If you were aware of light ahead, or were able to grope your way towards the light, the outcome may be less bleak than you thought. Stars or moon in the sky symbolize hope, and the beginning of more positive thinking.

Drowning

This dream could refer to an aspect of your life that you wish to hide. On the other hand, you may be drowning in a sea of problems. Or could you be drowning in self-pity? To watch someone else drown is a reflection of your own difficulties.

Adultery
(see RELATIONSHIPS, p88)
Blood
(see BODY, p63)
Jaws
(see BODY, p64)
Marsh
(see LANDSCAPE, p81)

Earthquake

External influences may cause this dream – a sudden noise, or a heavy vehicle passing. If such influences are excluded, the sensation of the earth moving beneath your feet could suggest insecurity in waking life (see page 36). If cracks appear in the earth it may be a warning that you are under extreme pressure.

Enemy

Often this dream relates to the 'enemy within', an element of your own personality that is inhibiting progress. It could represent a sexual fear, and carry a strong suggestion that you examine your attitude to sex carefully. If it is an outside force, or person, it could still reflect on your own personality. The person indicated in your dream may possess distasteful characteristics that you wish to erase in yourself.

Execution/Executioner

The 'executioner' could be someone who has dealt a 'final blow' to a relationship. Witnessing an execution is a violent experience, but the dream could have a simple meaning. Perhaps there is someone, or some thing that must be ruthlessly cut out of your life before you can make progress? If you were the victim, this could symbolize strong feelings of guilt.

Dream on, dream on of bloody deeds and death

William Shakespeare,
King Richard III

Fight

A dream that can sometimes represent change. How the fight developed may indicate how beneficial the change will be. It is also a dream of aggression, and could suggest that you become more assertive. Perhaps you should 'put up a fight' for something – or someone.

Gallows

Hanging on the gallows is often considered a dream of opposite meaning, indicating good fortune ahead. However, this can be a frightening dream (see page 21), and could reflect feelings of guilt.

Illness

Relate the illness carefully to your own state of mind. Perhaps you feel in need of a little pampering at the moment, and see yourself in the role of an invalid. If this is a recurring dream, it may be advisable to have a medical check-up.

Killing

A violent dream, but not necessarily a negative one. The dream killing may suggest something, or someone, you need to remove from your life. The dead person will always represent you (see 'Corpse', MORTALITY, page 83), so is there a trait of yours that needs eliminating?

Knife

Freud considered the knife, and all weapons, to be phallic symbols (see page 44). The knife is also related to violence, so what you were doing with it is important. Were you attacking someone? Or were you being attacked yourself? On the other hand, the dream may relate to a particular habit you are trying to 'cut out'.

Operation

A dream of a hospital operation seldom refers to a waking ailment. However, if you are worried, a medical check-up is no bad thing. The removal of something harmful is indicated, and the dream could imply that a psychological problem needs resolving A military operation may relate to something you are planning, or to your work.

Pain

If you experienced pain in your dream, there is a strong possibility that cramp, or indigestion may have been responsible (see page 39). However, dreams do sometimes signal symptoms of illness before they are diagnosed. So if you are in any doubt, have a medical check-up.

Punishment

To dream of being punished may reveal feelings of guilt. Or were you punishing yourself for a misdemeanour that is largely in your imagination? The dream could be commenting on past relationships with parents or teachers.

Shooting

Guns, according to Freud, are unmistakable sexual symbols. The dream could also represent an anxiety to be accurate, or 'on target'. Or it may suggest feelings of deep anger, in which case who, or what you were shooting at is of particular importance. If you were the target, perhaps you are blaming yourself unduly for something?

Wound

The dream wound may represent a psychological 'hurt'. If it was healing well, your emotional 'recovery' seems assured. But if it was festering, it is important to discover exactly what it symbolizes in your waking life, and to deal with it quickly.

Transport

Brake
(see ACTIVITY OBJECTS, p60)
Parking
(see ENVIRONMENT, p75)
Traffic
(see ENVIRONMENT, p75)

Aeroplane

If you were piloting the aeroplane, it could be an omen for unusual achievement in some waking enterprise. If you were a passenger, it may indicate that you were 'flying high' on someone else's achievement. Or were you, perhaps, being 'taken for a ride'? Watching aircraft dropping bombs, or in combat, could indicate a temporary emotional disturbance.

Hearse

A dream of opposite meaning. A hearse may indicate a psychological 'journey', with the promise of new experiences and increased knowledge. If you rode with the driver, you are about to accept new responsibilities. If a hearse came for you and you sent it away, you may not yet be ready to face those responsibilities (see also 'Funeral', MORTALITY, page 84).

Railway

If you were a passenger on the railway, your dream journey may be reflecting your progress in life. Were you without a ticket? Did you miss – or nearly miss – the train? Or was your journey uncomplicated? Dreaming of a steam railway suggests nostalgia, while trains entering tunnels symbolize sexual intercourse.

Rolls-Royce

An international status symbol, and usually an auspicious omen. If you dreamt of a Rolls-Royce, things may be looking up for you! (see also 'Colin's Dream', page 56).

Wheel

The wheel represents the 'mystic circle', a symbol of the self as a whole. How the wheel was turning may suggest how much control you have over your own life. If the wheel was in need of repair, it could indicate the need for more energy and endeavour.

Yacht

A yacht can be a status symbol. The more luxurious the yacht, the more you may be aiming for the 'high life'. But are you sure you are not being carried away by ideas of grandeur? If the yacht sailed away and left you on the shore, it could suggest a parting.

Glossary

alpha (rhythm, or brainwaves) normal activity of the *conscious* brain, consisting of 'oscillations' with a frequency of 8 to 13 hertz (cycles per second)

conscious (mind) having the mental faculties in an active and waking state.

delta (rhythm, or brainwaves) slow activity of the *unconscious* brain, consisting of deep oscillations having a frequency of 0.5 – 3 hertz (cycles per second)

ego part of the *conscious* mind, having a sense of individuality and being most conscious of 'self'.

id the instinctive impulses of the individual, forming part of the *unconscious* mind.

Lucid dreaming (see page 35) Stephen LaBerge is founder of the Lucidity Institute in California. For enquiries about his workshops, courses, books, etc. contact The Lucidity Institute, 2555 Park Blvd., Suite 2, Palo Alto, California 94306,USA. Tel: 001 415 321 9969. Fax: 001 415 321 9967. Books and lucidity products are available in the UK from: Life Tools, Sunrise House, Hulley Road, Macclesfield, Cheshire SK10 2LP. Tel: 01625 502602.

unconscious (mind) describes the mental processes of which a person is not aware, but which have a powerful effect on his or her attitudes and behaviour. The Freudian theory presumes that these processes are activated by desires, fears and memories which would be unacceptable to the conscious mind and are therefore repressed.

Bibliography

Barrett, David, *The Encyclopedia of Prediction* (Acropolis Books, 1992)

Brook, Stephen, *The Oxford Book of Dreams* (Oxford University Press, 1983)

Clifton, F. (ed) *The Faber Book of Anecdotes* (faber and faber, 1985)

Empson, Jacob, *Sleep and Dreaming* (faber and faber, 1989)

Fontana, David, *The Secret Language of Dreams* (Duncan Baird Publishers, 1994)

Fordham, Frieda, *An Introduction to Jung's Psychology* (Penguin Books, 1953)

Freud, Sigmund, *The Interpretation of Dreams* (Penguin Books,1991)

Hobbs, Richard, *Odilon Redon* (Macmillan, 1977)

Howatson, M.C. (ed) *The Oxford Companion to Classical Literature* (Oxford University Press, 1989)

Lucie-Smith, Edward, *Symbolist Art* (Thames and Hudson, 1972)

Mallon, Brenda, *Children Dreaming* (Penguin Books, 1989)

Morris, Desmond, *Catwatching* (Jonathan Cape, 1986)

Mountford, C.P. (text), Roberts, Ainslie (paintings) *The Dreamtime* (Art Australia, 1965)

Parker, Julia and Derek, *Dreaming* (Chancellor Press, 1993)

Thomas, Keith, *Religion and the Decline of Magic* (Penguin Books, 1991)

Walker, Stephen, *Animal Thought* (Routledge & Kegan Paul, 1983)

Index